PRADA

VALENTINO

VIVIENNE WESTWOOD and MALCOLM McLAREN
WITCHES

PRESENTATION DE LA COLLECTION

VALENTINO BOUTIQUE

PRINTEMPS - ETE 1995
DIMANCHE 16 OCTOBRE 1994 A 12H30
SALLE DELORME
LE CARROUSEL DU LOUVRE
99 RUE DE RIVOLI - 75001 PARIS

Monsieur Iain R. Webb

SECTEUR **B**   RANG **A 9**

R.S.V.P. VALENTINO 17/19 AVENUE MONTAIGNE 75008 PARIS TEL. 47.23.64.61
NOUS VOUS DEMANDONS D'AVOIR L'AMABILITE DE PRESENTER CETTE INVITATION A L'ENTREE

Yohji Yamamoto

103 grand street 10013 ny newyork tel(212)966-9066
155 rue saint-martin 75003 paris tel(1)42-78-94-11
2-2-43 higashi shinagatox shinagawa-ku tokyo tel(03)5463-1500

March 2015

Iain R Webb F/L
BA1

GILES ★

Autumn / Winter 2009
Monday 23rd February 2009
17.45pm

The Milk Factory
7 Wakefield Street, London WC1N 1PG

new look   TONI&GUY   CRYSTAL LIZED   MAC

INVITATION
STRICTLY
PERSONAL

FRONT ROW FASHION FREAK!
Best wishes
Iain R x

Published in 2014 by Goodman
An imprint of the Carlton Publishing Group
20 Mortimer Street
London W1T 3JW

10 9 8 7 6 5 4 3 2 1

A CIP catalogue record for this book is available from the British Library.

ISBN 978 1 84796 084 9

Printed in China

Note: All entries on the following pages are ready-to-wear womenswear,
unless otherwise indicated.

Previous page: Giles Deacon, Autumn/Winter 2009–10
Above: Paul Smith, Spring/Summer 2006

INVITATION STRICTLY PERSONAL

40 YEARS OF FASHION SHOW INVITES

IAIN R. WEBB

FOREWORD BY ANNA SUI

GOODMAN

Contents

Foreword by Anna Sui

I certainly spend a lot of time and effort thinking up new ideas for my bi-yearly fashion show invitations. For me, the trick is to allude to the theme of the collection, without giving away too much.

I'm very involved with all the details; the artwork and graphics, the weight of the card stock, the printing effects, the envelope colour, even which postage stamp to use. All aspects help tell the story by creating visual imagery around the collection.

I've always been a big collector of paper ephemera. It started out as a box of magazine clippings I saved under my bed as a kid growing up in Detroit. Now it practically fills a whole closet! I call it my "Genius Files". I refer to them almost every day. I'm still constantly adding things; making Xeroxes from library books, printing out images from the Internet, ripping out pages from magazines, saving postcards, snapshots, invitations, handbills from rock concerts. These nostalgic artifacts always inspire, and can transport me in a very emotional way.

Invitation Strictly Personal is a glorious archive of a particularly ingenious creative niche that may never have been properly documented before. These are the things the general public never sees. It's certainly an inspirational resource for fans of fashion, but also to anyone interested in design, graphics and pop culture history. Iain R. Webb has stylishly curated this splendid collection that is great fun to browse through. It's a wonderful addition to my personal library; one that I will be referring to often…

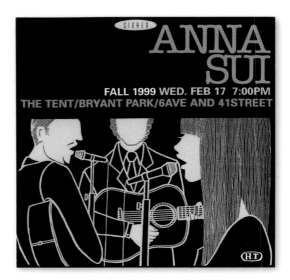

Gimbel Brothers, 1928

Lucien Lelong, undated

Lucien Lelong, undated

Introduction

"Does anyone have an invitation?" shrieks a harassed PR person from behind a wire fence. On the wrong side of the fence, *outside*, the crowd surges forward and in response, in unison, hands thrust in the air waving the coveted invite.

For anyone who has never attended a fashion show by a hot designer-of-the-moment it is hard to fathom the madness that can turn the heads of seemingly intelligent, rational people. The desperation in the desire to see the latest collection is palpable. Getting the priceless invitation is one thing; getting into the show, be it in New York, London, Milan or Paris, is quite another. Unless you are triple A-list worthy like US *Vogue* editor Anna Wintour, who accessorizes her outfits with besuited minders and thereby seems to drift miraculously through the crowd, gaining entrance can be a game of strategy, steely nerves and sheer willpower. Even top editors can have a fight on their hands as the late, great Liz Tilberis, editor of British *Vogue* (1987–1992) found out when she was once forced to battle her way through a tiny gap in a large fence along with *tout* Paris to gain access to a fashion show by Jean Paul Gaultier. Tilberis not only outmanoeuvred the heaving crowd, she also clobbered a couple of particularly officious bouncers along the way. When Tilberis returned to *Vogue*, legend has it that her team hung a pair of boxing gloves decorated with Chanel's double-C logo above her desk.

This apocryphal tale highlights the quandary faced by designers who want to create a buzz about their shows but also need to get the right designer-bedecked bums on the front-row seats. Iconic black-and-white photographs of early shows at Chanel and Dior invariably feature guests packed tightly into every available space. In 1976 retailer Joseph Ettedgui staged a fashion show in London's Embassy nightclub. His brother Franklin remembers how "we invited far too many people and they all turned up. There was chaos. The police had to control the crowds. Many prominent guests and press didn't get in."

Yet, as with most things in fashion, this scenario was nothing new. In 1914 a journalist mocked the hysteria surrounding a fashion show, describing how guests were swept up in a "delirium of dressing". Another report at that time likened a fashion show to "a music hall extravaganza", pre-empting Ossie Clark's crazy fashion happening at the Royal Court Theatre by half a century.

It wasn't always thus.

In the eighteenth century, before the press got a look in, the dresses would go to the client. Dressmakers would visit society women in their homes to make fittings for a gown while dolls dressed in small-scale replicas of the new fashions would be sent to clients in far-flung destinations. By the end of the nineteenth century, fashion houses started to create biannual collections and clients were invited to visit the couture houses to see the latest designs worn by live models. The mood at these *maisons de couture* was intimate, with salons decorated with gilded mirrors and lavish furnishings. Couturiers would often talk clients through the various ensembles on show. Although as far back as the seventeenth-century court fashions were reported in journals alongside illustrated fashion plates, it was not until the early twentieth century that the press would report on an official fashion calendar.

The fashion world works in it's own strange time continuum. Ready-to-wear shows are presented six months in advance (Spring/Summer showings the previous September/October; Autumn/Winter showings in February/March), while the couture showings are presented on season (Spring/Summer in January and Autumn/Winter in July). Menswear presentations are also shown six months in advance in January and July, with pre-collections shown between seasons to ensure clothes are continually being delivered to stores.

As fashion historians continue to debate who invented the mini-skirt (Mary Quant or André Courrèges are the designers usually caught in the fray), it is equally difficult to pinpoint exactly when and who staged the first fashion show. Charles Frederick Worth, who arrived in Paris from London in 1840, is said to be the first couturier to use models to show off his designs, while English designer Lucile (Lady Duff Gordon) is most often credited with inventing the fashion show in London in 1900. It is believed she was the first to employ a raised platform (or catwalk) on which models posed in her showroom. In the summer Lucile held presentations, described as something between an elegant soirée and theatrical performance, in her garden.

When retailers and manufacturers originally attended shows, they did not buy actual dresses but would purchase the right to reproduce sample or prototype dresses known as *models*. This *model* often came with suggestions for fabrication, colourways and trimmings, although the couturier's original designs were invariably altered for

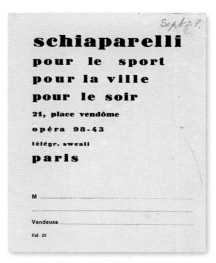

Schiaparelli, undated

Mainbocher, 1939

Jeanne Lanvin, 1950

Ossie Clark, A/W 1977, S/S 1978

Worlds End, A/W 1983

Karl Lagerfeld, A/W 1989–90

commercial reasons. In the 1930s formal registration was introduced along with a buyers entrance card that guaranteed the bearer would make a minimum order for which the price of admission was paid. American retailers such as Macy's, Gimbel Brothers and Bergdorf Goodman would unveil these newly imported designs a month or so later at large-scale events, with tickets sold to the general public who attended in their thousands.

Buyers and private clients were never invited to the same show. The top couture houses offered a sense of exclusivity with entry by invitation only. In the early years these were usually handwritten but later engraved cards became popular as if for a private party. Invited guests might be as few as 20 and refreshments were provided as shows often lasted for more than an hour and a half. Today fashion shows can be over in seven minutes. Down the decades designers have dressed up the fashion show with cocktails, light suppers and lavish black-tie dinners. In today's world of instant Instagrammed images and live-streamed fashion reports, it is hard to imagine a time when photographers were not welcome at fashion shows and even sketching was not permitted. Some designers were so protective of their designs that they even employed private detectives to follow buyers who had legitimately purchased designs to make sure they did not sell them to copyists.

Much of the innovation that has occurred in the fashion industry did so at the dawn of the twentieth century. Press shows were initiated in 1923 at the house of Jean Patou and the press has become an important tool in selling the designer's dream. In an effort to make the journalists feel special, invitations were limited and designers would seat fashion editors alongside celebrities, a strategy still popular today. Guests were often provided with champagne and presented with favours such as gifts of perfume. Special programmes not only provided information about the collection but also acted as notebooks with tiny pencils attached. Such devices have become an essential part of the designer's promotional package, which can include other freebie gifts such as show soundtracks, make-up and, before the advent of the mobile telephone, even pre-paid phone-cards. An on-seat goodie bag is now almost de rigueur and the press has become as much a part of the show as the models on the catwalk, with other journalists documenting the fashions worn by the front-row fashion pack.

Fashion depends on looking forward, but while the sensational shows of John Galliano and Alexander McQueen have been viewed as cutting edge, the notion of the fashion show as a spectacular and theatrical production began with designers such as Lucile, Paul Poiret, Jeanne Paquin, Jeanne Lanvin and Lucien Lelong in the first half of the twentieth century, who mounted elaborate performances in theatres, gardens and country houses which included models appearing on horseback, frolicking in ornamental fountains or acting out slight dramatic narratives. In 1938 Elsa Schiaparelli introduced the idea of a themed collection with her "Circus" show that included clowns, jugglers, elephants, monkeys and trained dogs. Fashion shows are often a hybrid of commerce and theatre.

In the 1960s Mary Quant used go-go dancers in her shows, although this was not a new innovation as Paquin had previously presented shows featuring tango dancers and celebrity dance duo Irene and Vernon Castle. In the 1980s Bodymap enlisted avant-garde ballet star Michael Clark on their catwalk, while in the 1990s Geoffrey Beene teamed up with the New York City Ballet.

The purpose of a fashion show can be as diverse as the invitations that herald them. Some designers create a specific catwalk collection to garner rave reviews while another commercial collection, aimed at buyers, hangs on racks back in the showroom. Costly haute couture shows are mostly used to promote a designer's fragrance or the brand itself, the astronomical cost of staging a show being offset against the valuable free publicity.

Location can also play a key role. While the British Fashion Council offers the mod-con corporate comforts of the official London Fashion Week tented venue, currently in the grounds of historical Somerset House, New York's Mercedes-Benz Fashion Week is located at the Lincoln Center, and purpose-built venues are offered in Paris (the Carrousel du Louvre) and Milan (the Fiera), many designers still prefer to present their collections in more idiosyncratic settings. These can range from uninviting and shambolic (a meat market or derelict postal depot) to tourist attraction grandiose (the Royal Albert Hall or Opera Garnier). Designers have shown their designs in nightclubs, art galleries and fancy restaurants, even their homes. Giorgio Armani built a catwalk in the basement of his Milan home while Karl Lagerfeld once presented his collection for Chanel in Coco's private apartment at the Ritz Paris.

Marc Jacobs, S/S 1996

Chanel, S/S 1996

Gianni Versace, A/W 1997–98

Christian Lacroix, S/S 1998

Helmut Lang, circa 1992

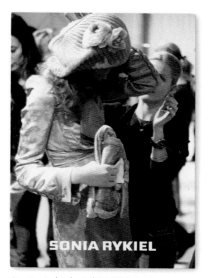

Sonia Rykiel, A/W 2006–7

Fashion works in extremes, so while McQueen, Galliano and Gaultier (who feature repeatedly in this book due to their groundbreaking efforts and extraordinary vision) have created bigger and bolder stadium-style shows more akin to rock concerts, other designers have yearned for the exclusivity of yesteryear salon shows. When Tom Ford returned to the fashion industry in 2010 after taking time out to direct *A Single Man*, he hand-picked key fashion industry players from his elite circle of friends to see his new collection, modelled by other celebrity friends and narrated by the man himself. The show was so intimate that Ford did not even mail out invitations but instead had his team telephone his guests to invite them personally. Not surprisingly, this became the most talked about show of the season.

Designers are always trying to present their collections in new and exciting ways. Young designers such as Meadham Kirchhoff can act as game changers. For their Spring/Summer 2013 menswear collection they invited their guests to a "show/presentation/whatever". In fact, their curated staging might best be described as an installation – think Tracey Emin's *My Bed* occupied by pretty punk boys wearing chiffon dresses with fluorescent trainers and matching hair.

The debate surrounding the purpose and effectiveness of the catwalk show versus the vast cost and production headaches is a continuing conundrum that designers face. Who really needs to see their show?

In 1998 designer Helmut Lang embraced the future when he presented his collection solely via the Internet for all to see (press and buyers were invited to view his designs privately in his showroom at a later date). As the digital revolution has exploded in recent years, so the online experience has become important in a designer's repertoire, be it live-streamed catwalk shows or the total interactive experience offered by Burberry designer Christopher Bailey, who has harnessed social media and made it a core part of the brand. Bailey has even engineered it so online guests are just one click away from purchasing directly from the Burberry Prorsum catwalk.

But what is the purpose of the invitation itself? For some designers it is purely functional, used to inform guests of the venue and time of show. For others it can offer clues to the mood of the collection with a single evocative photograph or a complex package of curios. A designer might employ words or graphics to tell their story or rely on an emotional reaction to a colour, fabric or object. Sometimes they can be playful, like Vier 5's caricatures of Suzy Menkes and Carine Roitfeld, or purposefully provocative, such as Andrew Groves' flaming cross or McQueen's slashed flesh. The invitation provides endless possibilities for a designer to reflect the essence of their ethos or brand, from the purist approach of Calvin Klein to the charming decorative touch of Meadham Kirchhoff. While John Galliano will personally curate a treasure trove of items that come together as a visual teaser for the collection, a designer such as Betsy Johnson just wants to have fun with her show invitation, mimicking the saucy girliness and gaiety in store on her catwalk. Isaac Mizrahi might include humorous asides alongside dress descriptions in his shownotes, while Michael Kors will offer purely the bare bones of his inspirations. The different ways in which designers choose to present themselves, be it Sonia Rykiel's classic black-and-white likeness or Patrick Kelly's fabulously flamboyant portrait, is revealing in itself. Invitations can add mystery to a forthcoming presentation or share inspiration, offer a backstory or act as a backdrop. An invitation often drip-feeds imagery that puts the clothes on the catwalk into a greater context.

Invitations are a little piece of fashion history. I have curated this book from my personal collection and the much-loved collections of my front-row colleagues. It is not intended as a definitive compendium but is instead a unique assemblage of fabulous iconic fashion moments that offer a glimpse into the world of the international catwalk show. Many of these invitations will only have been seen previously by those fortunate enough to attend the show.

And yet, with the advent of social media, the collections are now available for everyone to experience. Canny designers and their creative teams offer backstage sneak previews of hair and make-up while teenage models tweet selfies with their model mates. Guests Instagram images of the venue, their seating placement, the back of an editor's head, anything that might share their sense of excitement, before the show has even begun. Even invitations are posted on Facebook. However, nothing can replace that feeling when an envelope drops through your letterbox containing an invitation bearing your name underneath the words: Invitation Strictly Personal.

Vier5, S/S 2011

Maison Martin Margiela, A/W 2010–11

Andrew Groves, A/W 1998–99

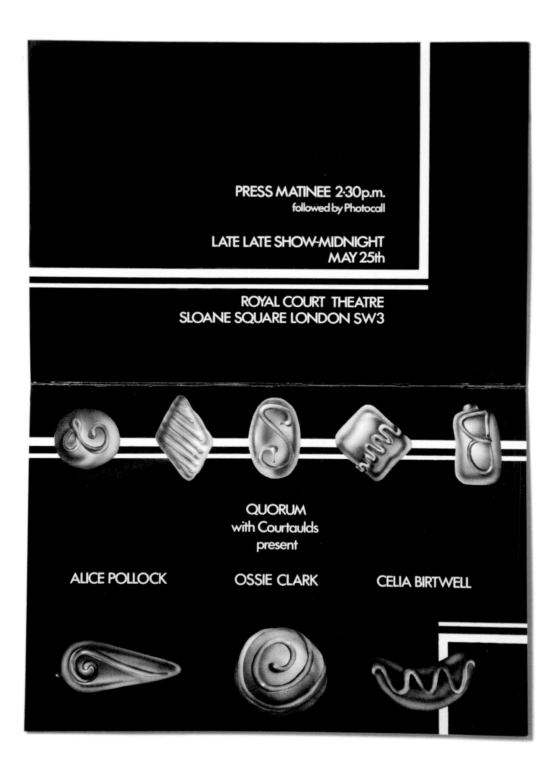

PRESS MATINEE 2·30p.m.
followed by Photocall

LATE LATE SHOW-MIDNIGHT
MAY 25th

ROYAL COURT THEATRE
SLOANE SQUARE LONDON SW3

QUORUM
with Courtaulds
present

ALICE POLLOCK   OSSIE CLARK   CELIA BIRTWELL

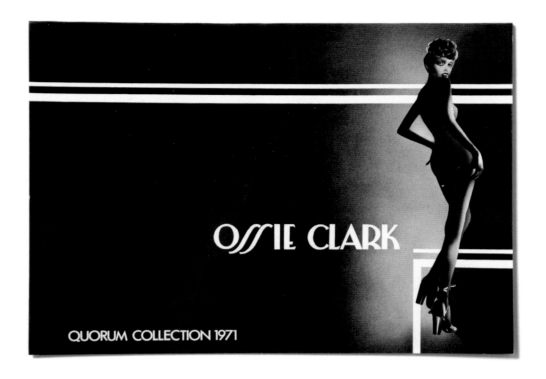

OSSIE CLARK

QUORUM COLLECTION 1971

Show
Quorum Collection
1971

Date/Time
25th May 1971
2.30pm and Midnight

Place
Royal Court Theatre
Sloane Square
London

Format/Size
Card (unfolded)
29.5cm x 20.5cm
(11½in x 8in)

Quorum

Quorum was the forward-thinking label of designer Alice Pollock, launched in 1964. In the next few decades it became a showcase for upcoming designers, including husband-and-wife team Ossie Clark and Celia Birtwell, who featured in this fashion show. The choice of venue was telling, as the Royal Court Theatre had a reputation for being a hothouse for edgy playwrights such as John Osborne and Joe Orton.

This chocolate-box invitation (the show was sponsored by Black Magic) hinted at indulgence, fashion as pure pleasure, and that is exactly what the invited guests were treated to. The late show, which did not start until after 2am, was a hedonistic mix of satin suits and floral-printed frocks, with models Gala Mitchell, Alice Ormsby-Gore and Patti d'Arbanville camping it up to a soundtrack of R&B hits. Guests, who included pop stars, photographers and painters, remember the experience being more akin to a wild party than designers displaying their new clothing ranges.

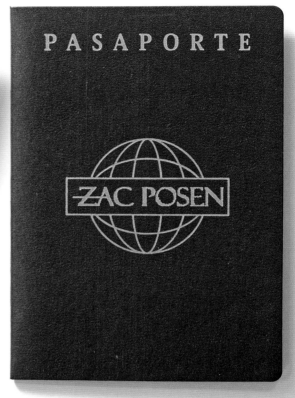

The Secretary of State
of the United States of America
hereby request all whom it may concern to permit the citizen/
national of the United States named herein pass
without delay or hindrance and in case of need to
give all lawful aid and protection.

le Secrétaire d'Etat
des Etats-Unis d'Amerique
prie pas les presents toutes autorites comprentes de laisser passer
le ditoyen ou ressortissant des Etats-Unis titulaire de present passeport,
sans delai ni difficulte et, en cas de besoin, de lui accorder
toute aide et protection legitimes

Name:
ZAC POSEN
Purpose of visit:
2003 SPRING/SUMMER/COLLECTION
Date of arrival:
THURSDAY 13 FEBRUARY, 2003
Destination:
LOTUS 409 WEST 14TH STREET
NYC
Additional activities:
COCKTAILS 11PM – 1AM
Contact:
RSVP MANDATORY 212.226.6123
Authority:
MARK BAKER PRO. & JEFFREY JAH
COMM.
Sponsor: QUADRIGA WWW.SUPERFUND.COM

Zac Posen

The venue for Zac Posen's aftershow party was described by *New York* magazine
as an "emporium for the suits and the scantily clad". In its review of the multi-level
nightspot, it also categorized the Lotus club-goers as "unfunky". The fit with Mr Posen
was pretty good because, while the 22-year-old designer was precociously rocking
the New York fashion scene, he had always been pure Hollywood. Even though
ingénue Natalie Portman was a front-row stalwart at his shows (including this one,
staged in the gilded historic spendour of Gotham Hall, built in 1922), the designer's
aesthetic has more in common with costume designers Adrian and Travis Banton,
who between them dressed Rita Hayworth, Betty Grable and Marlene Dietrich. For
this collection, Posen offered a selection of flirty 1940s-inspired gowns. His line-up
of stellar international supermodels included Natalia Vodianova, Karolina Kurkova,
Mariacarla Boscono, Anouck Lepère and Naomi Campbell. The passport invitation
gave us entry into the world of Zac Posen.

Show
Spring/Summer
2003

Date/Time
13th February 2003
11pm–1am

Place
Lotus
409 West 14th Street
New York

Format/Size
Passport (folded)
13cm x 9cm
(5in x 3½in)

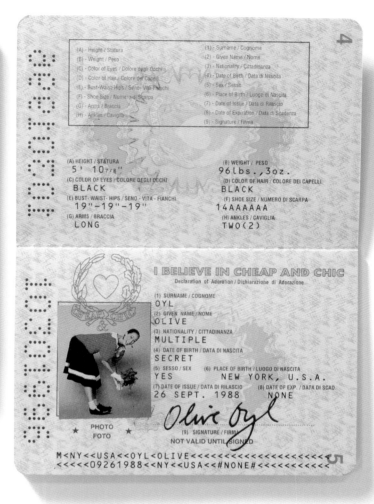

Show
Spring/Summer
1997

Date/Time
30th October 1996
9am

Place
CFDA Pavilion
Bryant Park
20 West 40th Street
New York

Format/Size
Passport (folded)
13cm x 9cm
(5in x 3½in)

Moschino Cheap and Chic

This invitation was designed as a 16-page passport for the beanpole cartoon character Olive Oyl, listing her measurements as 19" – 19" – 19" and her shoe size as 14AAAAAA. The photograph pictured model Pat Cleveland, dressed as a doppelganger in an uncanny resemblance. Underneath "Important Information", one entry in the passport recommended: "Since our show is at 9am we advise that you arrive in the city the day before. That way you get enough rest to feel fresh enough to remember to bring your happy face along", while another warned: "Photocopies of this invitation are not valid, even if they are fancy colour copies. We really don't care if you doodle all over this invitation or dribble your cappuccino on it." As ever, humour was uppermost, with the fashion house playfully teasing its guests: "Some people may be fortunate enough to be invited to more than one event at the same time. We advise that they come to our show".

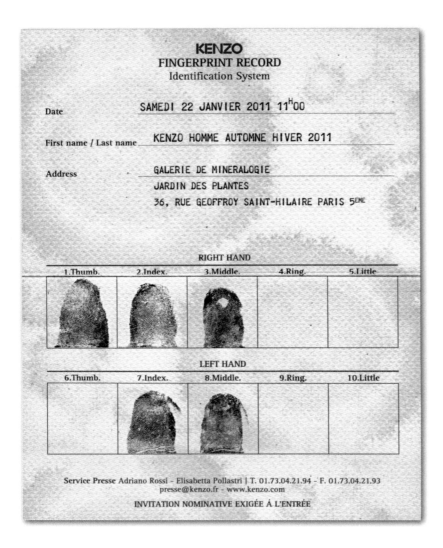

KENZO

FINGERPRINT RECORD

Identification System

Date   SAMEDI 22 JANVIER 2011 11^{H}00

First name / Last name   KENZO HOMME AUTOMNE HIVER 2011

Address   GALERIE DE MINERALOGIE

           JARDIN DES PLANTES

           36, RUE GEOFFROY SAINT-HILAIRE PARIS 5EME

RIGHT HAND

1.Thumb.	2.Index.	3.Middle.	4.Ring.	5.Little

LEFT HAND

6.Thumb.	7.Index.	8.Middle.	9.Ring.	10.Little

Service Presse Adriano Rossi - Elisabetta Pollastri | T. 01.73.04.21.94 - F. 01.73.04.21.93
presse@kenzo.fr - www.kenzo.com

INVITATION NOMINATIVE EXIGÉE Á L'ENTRÉE

Kenzo

The invitation offered a clue to the theme of the show as designer Antonio Marais renamed the Kenzo HQ on rue Vivienne as Metropolitan Investigator. The water-stained identity card appeared to come from another era, perhaps that of Arthur J. Raffles, gentleman thief, Christopher Foyle or even Professor Plum. The mood of the collection was certainly grounded in British heritage with the usual style suspects on the catwalk: heathery plaid and floral suits, military stripe trousers, Fair Isle waistcoats and a down-on-its-luck windowpane check cardigan that had the look of a shabbily patched favourite. There were also eccentric idiosyncratic touches that would have stood out in any parade: bow ties and outdoorsy tweeds and a kilt worn with a dinner suit teamed with a bowler hat. And the question of identity was still in flux at the end of the show when Marais himself appeared in cosy tweeds and knit, looking as much a beloved boarding-school house master as an international designer.

Show
Menswear
Autumn/Winter
2011–12

Date/Time
22nd January 2011
11am

Place
Galerie de Minéralogie et de Géologie
Jardin des Plantes
36 rue Geoffroy-Saint-Hilaire
Paris

Format/Size
Identity card (unfolded)
18cm x 14cm
(7in x 5½in)

16   IDENTITY

ACADÉMIE
de *FASHION WEEKLY*

DÉPARTEMENT
de *PR*

PRESSE

HEDI SLIMANE-TORTELLA

43361686 FAX 43371587

ANNÉE SCOLAIRE 199..... - 199.....

CARTE D'IDENTITÉ ÉTUDIANT

Je, soussigné, **JOSE LEVY A PARIS**

certifie que M *CLARK* Prénom : *Adrian*

né (e) le .... 19....., à .... Dép¹ ....

Nationalité ....

LA SORBONNE SALLE DES AUTORITES

demeurant ....

17 RUE DE LA SORBONNE PARIS VEME

est élève dans mon établissement en qualité d ....

17H30 JEUDI 30 JANVIER

A .... le .... 199.....

Signature du Titulaire   Signature du Chef d'Etablissement .

ENSEIGNEMENT SUPÉRIEUR AGRÉÉ POUR LA SÉCURITÉ SOCIALE

C.P.A.M. de .... Nº ÉCOLE ....

Show
Menswear
Autumn/Winter
1992–93

Date/Time
30th January 1992
5.30pm

Place
Salle des Autorités
La Sorbonne
17 rue de la Sorbonne
Paris

Format/Size
Identity card (unfolded)
16cm x 12cm
(6¼in x 4¾in)

Jose Levy

For this show at the Sorbonne, designer Levy presented a line-up of geeky Parisian intellectuals, just the type who might carry the student identity card used for the invitation. The look was stylish but laid-back, with Levy exploring the notion of a man who cares more for reading than ready-to-wear. That meant seductively insouciant baggy suits, roomy raincoats, collegiate scarves, spectacles and the classic beatnik beret. Levy's trademark look is effortlessly French. The designer has also designed men's collections for Cacharel, Nina Ricci and Emanuel Ungaro and has since turned his hand to furniture, home furnishings and decorative art.

This invitation lists Hedi Slimane (then Slimane-Tortella) as press contact. Slimane is now one of the most revered designers in the world and is credited with reshaping the look of contemporary menswear. He is currently creative director at Saint Laurent, where he is shaking things up just as Yves did in his youth on the Left Bank.

E2

Michèle Mariot and Olivier Chatenet began designing together in the late 1980s before producing one-of-a-kind outfits under the E2 label. Their method of customizing, remaking and revamping antique pieces from YSL, Gucci, Chloé and even Madame Grès was a concept shared by the Imitation of Christ label in New York. The WANTED image featured on the poster was pertinent as the duo's one-off offerings (under occupation the pair listed themselves as "Fashion dealers") were definitely desired by the fashion industry, who were tiring of the production-line antics of the giant corporations, be they the heavyweight luxury goods houses or the fast turnover value brands. The husband-and-wife team immediately developed a cult following, staging this first show in the courtyard entrance of their own apartment block, with several of their fans, including supermodel Linda Evangelista and Virginie Viard, head of design at Chanel, modelling on their catwalk. Evangelista wore a black reworked Chanel suit in the show. Other looks featured embroidered flowers.

Show
Haute Couture
Autumn/Winter
2003

Date/Time
8th July 2003
6pm

Place
15 rue Martel
Paris

Format/Size
Poster
59.5cm x 39.5cm
(23½in x 15½in)

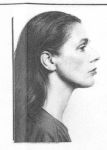

Alexander McQueen

In association with sponsor American Express, Alexander McQueen staged a retrospective-style show of favourite catwalk moments billed as "a celebration of five years of the Centurion Card" (aka the Black Card). It was the first time the designer had shown in London for three years as he now presented his collections in Paris. The industrial Earls Court exhibition space was transformed into a luxurious ballroom lit with chandeliers. Models paraded inside a giant glass box mirrored on the inside that McQueen had first featured in his "Asylum" show of Spring/Summer 2001. The effect was eerie and disconcerting.

The show began with a sensational duet by punk ballet dancer Michael Clark and Kate Moss. Looks dating from his 1995 "Highland Rape" show were reworked in black while the final white outfit was worn by a model standing alone beneath a shower of rain. An auction of Black Art by the designer's friends, including Sam Taylor-Wood (now Taylor-Johnson) and Tracey Emin, followed the show. McQueen also designed a limited-edition card with proceeds benefiting an HIV/AIDS charity.

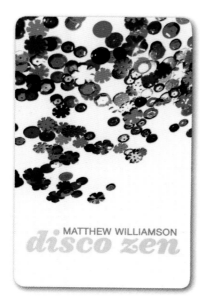

Matthew Williamson

Williamson's debut show only a year earlier had been one of those moments that changed the fashion landscape. Titled "Electric Angels", it had featured only 14 outfits – a mix of brightly coloured separates. While the designer's collections grew in size over time, he maintained his penchant for what he calls "kaleidoscopic colour", embellishment and print, so this invitation featuring a scattering of colourful sequin paillettes and iridescent metallic foil lettering suited perfectly the designers core brand profile. Even the title, Disco Zen, married two elemental references in Williamson's work: the energetic pizzazz of celebrity-laced nightclub culture combined with his clientele's free-spirited, laid-back approach to glamour. Helena Christensen closed the show wearing a sheer tulle dress embroidered with a firework design of multicoloured sequins that encapsulated the look perfectly. The outdoor venue alluded to nights spent under the moon, or perhaps a mirrorball.

Show
Spring/Summer
1999

Time/Date
28th September 1998
7.15pm

Place
Smithfields
Grand Avenue
London

Format/Size
Business card, plastic
8.5cm x 5.5cm
(3¼in x 2 in)

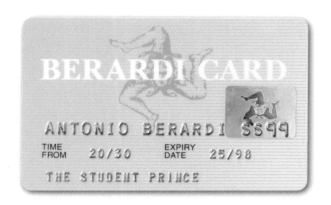

Show
Spring/Summer
1999

Date/Time
25th September 1998
8.30pm

Place
Royal Horticultural
Halls
80 Vincent Square
London

Format/Size
Credit card, plastic
5.5cm x 8.5cm
(2in x 3¼in)

Antonio Berardi

The title, "The Student Prince", gave a hint that Antonio Berardi would use the show to launch a new menswear line. It began with a group of well-toned male models dressed in variations on a quilted white fencing ensemble, followed by sailors in tight-fitting underwear and jaunty caps. These body-conscious outfits could have been designed specifically for sportsman David Beckham, who sat front row. Certainly, the sleek, sexy looks that followed would have suited his fiancée Victoria (Posh Spice) Adams, who sat with him. Both would no doubt have flexed the Berardi credit card. The mostly white collection pulled from the designer's continued inspirations, including sportswear and religious iconography. Cropped trouser suits were rapier thin while broderie lace dresses were pure as Catholic Communion frocks. Berardi added punk and ethnic elements, mini-kilts and slashed T-shirts, elaborate embroideries and sculptural basketweave. And for this showing, the drama was in the hairpieces that were twisted and teased into looks referencing both geisha and Ganesh.

John Galliano

By the time John Galliano had become a regular on the Paris Fashion Week schedule the fashion pack had come to expect something of a scavenger hunt across the capital just to locate the venue for his latest presentation. This season was no different. The playing card invitations caused much head scratching, were they part of a tarot pack? On entering the venue the answer was clear, as the front row took their seats on bales of hay in a circus-cum-gypsy encampment, with models doubling as showgirls, tumblers and fortune tellers. In a flurry of flamenco frills they walked on straw, with twinkling fairy lights hanging from the ceiling. On the soundtrack a ringmaster announced, "Ladies and Gentlemen, the Sensation of the Ages!" That included Helena Christensen with starbursts exploding from her corset, Nadja Auermann shimmying in a sliver of pink chiffon and a plume of ostrich feathers, and, Galliano himself with waist-length blond dreadlocks, followed by an authentic gypsy band.

Show
Spring/Summer
1997

Date/Time
10th October 1996
7.30pm

Place
Corner of rue Baron
Leroy and avenue
des Terroirs de
France
Paris

Format/Size
Playing card
8.5cm x 5.5cm
(3¼in x 2in)

Show
Spring/Summer
2005

Alexander McQueen

Date/Time
8th October 2004
8pm

Place
Palais Omnisports
de Paris-Bercy
8 boulevard de Bercy
Paris

Format/Size
Playing card
9cm x 6.5cm
(3½in x 2½in)

While the playing card invitation for Alexander McQueen's "It's Only a Game" show depicted a joker, it was the strategic board game of chess that inspired this presentation. Staged in a cavernous white studio, 36 models paraded to "Relax" and "Two Tribes" by Frankie Goes To Hollywood before lining up in six neat rows with military precision. The first look, a reworking of an Edwardian-style child's sailor suit, defined the romantic mood. Abbreviated crinolines, baby-doll dresses and half-mast trousers that alluded to childhood, and provocative bodysuits and moulded leather corsets-cum-surgical braces showcased the craftsmanship of McQueen's studio. With the last model in place, the auditorium faded to darkness for McQueen's twist-in-the-tail finale. As spotlights cast a checkerboard effect on the floor a computer intoned, "Now we start the game" and choreographed the models: "Bishop A2 to Queen C4", "Sacrificial Move" until "Checkmate". Game over, McQueen, wearing his signature low-slung jeans, took his bows to Elvis Presley singing "Suspicious Minds".

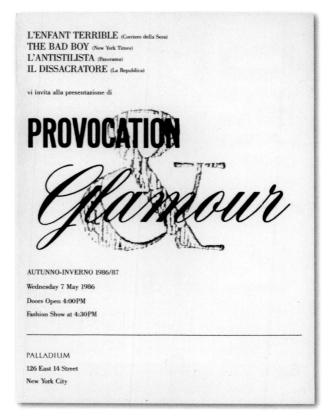

L'ENFANT TERRIBLE (Corriere della Sera)
THE BAD BOY (New York Times)
L'ANTISTILISTA (Panorama)
IL DISSACRATORE (La Republica)

vi invita alla presentazione di

PROVOCATION

Glamour

AUTUNNO-INVERNO 1986/87
Wednesday 7 May 1986
Doors Open 4:00PM
Fashion Show at 4:30PM

PALLADIUM
126 East 14 Street
New York City

Moschino

Throughout his career, Franco Moschino used his designs to "make jokes about fashion", favouring clever word play and slogans on his clothes, such as the hourglass jacket encircled with the words "WAIST OF MONEY" and another embroidered with "FULL OF CHIC!". While this show's title, "Provocation & Glamour", encapsulated his ethos perfectly, the invitation set the tone by listing descriptions of the designer – L'Enfant Terrible, The Bad Boy, etc. – culled from international newspapers.

There are some designers whose image is enmeshed with their ideology and from very early on Moschino was as much the brand as the clothes he designed. He controlled all aspects of his image, even featuring in his own advertising campaigns, including womenswear – in a blond wig – and childrenswear – dressed as a baby in a bonnet. In this photograph, he poses as a matinee idol. He relished the staging and art direction involved in putting a show together and once mused that, "I would like to be a movie director." In the downtown Manhattan nightclub Palladium, he was in an appropriate environment to parade his overtly stylized designs that drew inspiration from iconic gay imagery, from cowboys to leather queens.

Show
Autumn/Winter
1986–87

Date/Time
7th May 1986
4.30pm

Place
Palladium
126 East 14th Street
New York

Format/Size
Card
19cm x 14cm
(7½in x 5½in)

Bernstock Speirs

Show
Spring/Summer
1990

Date/Time
14th–17th October
1989

Place
British Designer Show
Olympia 2
Hammersmith Road
London

Format/Size
Card
20cm x 10.5cm
(7¾in x 4in)

With the prompt to "Act Sexy", hat designers Paul Bernstock and Thelma Speirs pose for photographer David Woolley. Their choice of outfits totally encapsulates the brand's fun and funky aesthetic – Mr Bernstock's patterned Lycra cycling shorts and anonymous-looking sweatshirt teamed with Cuban-heeled ankle boots and a sporty peak cap being a foil for the sequinned evening ensemble, peep-toe sandals and coiffed hairstyle favoured by Ms Speirs. The playfulness of this juxtaposition was evident in a collection that was a mixture of sporty, functional pieces and handmade couture designs. In the 1980s, the pair brought a sense of fun to the London collections and became the hot duo that designers turned to when accessorizing their catwalk shows – they have collaborated with Jean Paul Gaultier, Richard Nicoll and Peter Jensen, among others. They were immediately popular with pop stars such as Kylie Minogue. Their pose on the invitation highlights just how inseparable the pair are from each other as they are from the brand.

Stephen Jones

When Stephen Jones graduated from Saint Martin's School of Art, London, in 1979, he realized that he was never going to follow a conventional career plan. Jones was part of the New Romantic scene, which was centred around the Blitz nightclub, and was already making hats for his circle of friends, including singer Steve Strange. Audaciously, Jones opened a salon in the basement of PX, a boutique catering for the Blitz crowd, funding the venture by selling his car. The ambience of his salon was pure theatrical glamour – classical busts and chi-chi gilt furniture set against a backdrop of silver grey moiré. To publicize the store and his collection, Jones posed with his muse Kim Bowen, who would wear his more extraordinary creations as though she were pulling on a bobble hat. The mood was flamboyant, romantic and historical. Pete Ashworth, a friend of Jones who was achieving fame in the music industry, photographed this image.

Show
Promotional material

Date/Time
1980

Place
Basement, PX
Endell Street
London

Format/Size
Card
21cm x 15cm
(8¼in x 6in)

Show
Autumn/Winter
1983–84

Date/Time
20th March 1983
6.30pm

Place
Salle Sully
Palais du Louvre
Cour du Louvre
Paris

Format/Size
Card
15.5cm x 23cm
(6¼in x 9in)

Sonia Rykiel

Sonia Rykiel is one of France's most instantly recognizable fashion icons. Down the decades, the startling redhead has posed for photographers and artists, including Andy Warhol. Here, she was captured by Dominique Issermann. Rykiel is the very embodiment of a fashion designer, her work being totally intuitive. Originally she began designing for practical reasons – unable to find suitable maternity wear, she simply knitted herself dresses and sweaters. Championed by French *Elle*, she was soon heralded as the "Queen of Knitwear" by the powerful industry newspaper, *Women's Wear Daily*. Her easy, carefree designs captured the free-thinking spirit of the intellectuals who gathered on the Left Bank of Paris, where she opened her first boutique in 1968. By the time of this show, the designer had established an elegant, yet playful formula that earned her "Vintage Rykiel" headlines in the press. The black-and-white portrait by Issermann captures the designer's romantic, soft-focus mood. No doubt she was dreaming up her next collection.

> when johnny woke his
> hands & feet had been
> tied up, & he found
> his arms had been
> tattooed from the shoul-
> ders to the wrists.
>
> "& they're supposed
> to be my friends" he
> thought.
>
> boys will be boys.

John Richmond

John Richmond, who had been one half of trendy London design duo Richmond Cornejo in the early 1980s, launched his own label when he split from his partner Maria in 1987. With some designers it is hard to differentiate the creator from the clothes – such is the case with Richmond. This moody black-and-white portrait by Martin Brading shows him posing in his own designs, the embodiment of rock'n'roll, which is at the tattooed heart of his design ethos and now embedded in the John Richmond brand. His clothes have been worn by Axl Rose, Madonna and Mick Jagger. Tattoos have become part of the designer's lexicon – one of his early retail hits was a leather jacket that featured tattooed sleeves – and still feature as lavish embroideries or glittering crystal. The words printed on the greaseproof paper bag were by the designer, "trying to be Patti Smith". They say as much about the collection on offer as any description of the garments themselves ever could.

Show
Spring/Summer
1989

Date/Time
3rd–6th September 1988

Place
Olympia
Hammersmith Road
London

Format/Size
Greaseproof paper bag
28cm x 21cm
(11in x 8¼in)
Photograph
25.5cm x 20.5cm
(10in x 8¼in)

Show
Menswear
Spring/Summer
2012

Date/Time
21st September 2011
7pm

Place
One Mayfair
13A North Audley
Street
London

Format/Size
Card
21cm x 14.5cm
(8¼in x 5¾in)

Hardy Amies

This collection was part of a concerted effort by the brand established by Sir Hardy Amies in 1945 (he retired in 2001) to reposition itself to attract a younger clientele. In 1964, Amies published the *ABC of Men's Fashion*, which is now being reworked for a new generation as an online ABC blog featuring entries such as "D is for Double-breasted and Deckchair", "S is for Serpentine Swimming Club and The Savoy", where Amies presented his debut catwalk show in 1961.

Amies always wanted his shows to be special so he would have approved of this show, staged at the former St Mark's Church in London's Mayfair, where models paraded against the backdrop of a golden altar. Incumbent creative director Claire Malcolm offered silk jackets, satin shirts, comfy cardigans and formal blazers worn with T-shirts, twisted neckerchief and shorts, perhaps inspired by the portrait of Amies in St Tropez, 1952, on the invitation.

ENGLISHMAN IN PARIS

KATHARINE HAMNETT
SPRING/SUMMER '89 MENS COLLECTION

ARISTOCRACY DRESSING . INNOCENCE . QUALITY

OLD BOYS CLUB . SAVILLE ROW . INTEGRITY

THOROUGHBRED . CRICKET . POWERFUL & ECCENTRIC

SIMPLICITY . DECADENCE . ECLECTIC DRESSING

Katharine Hamnett

There has always been a moment when British designers decide that in an effort to reach an international audience the time is right for them to pack up bags at London Fashion Week and try their luck on the catwalks in Milan, Paris or New York. Throughout the 1980s this was the case with several top-rated designers, including Katharine Hamnett. Although the designer chose to stage this menswear show in the French capital, the look she presented couldn't have been more British.

While previously she had specialized in utilitarian clothing, for this collection, titled "Englishman in Paris", Hamnett was having a heritage moment, inspired by the traditions of menswear. Her progamme notes highlighted buzzwords including Saville Row (sic), Old Boys Club, Thoroughbred and Aristocracy Dressing. On her catwalk, this translated as double-breasted blazers, morning coats, high-waisted trousers held up with suspenders and Georgian-style rosebud-embroidered waistcoats. Hamnett acknowledged her French hosts by using Jean-Honoré Fragonard's *The Swing* for her invitation, alongside this über-cool portrait that was included in her press pack.

Show
Menswear
Spring/Summer
1989

Date/Time
4th September 1988
5.30pm

Place
Syndicat General des Fondeur
de France
2 rue de Bassano
Paris

Format/Size
Paper
29.5cm x 21cm
(11¾in x 8¼in)
Photograph
25cm x 20cm
10in x 8in

Kris Van Assche

This collection was all about the message between the seams. The Belgian designer literally sliced through sleek suits and filled the gaps with slogan sweatshirts that read, "Rugged, Rough 'N' Tough". Hoodies were joined to shirts, sweaters grafted together. Van Assche's muse is a rule breaker (even his shoes are a collage of a trainer and Derby lace-up), so appropriately he chose to call his collection "Choose Life", writ large on this poster-sized invite, a slogan originally printed on oversized T-shirts by designer Katharine Hamnett in 1983. This particular T-shirt proved a big hit when worn by the pop group Wham! It was also parodied by Frankie Goes To Hollywood. Other Hamnett slogans included "Ban Pollution", "Save The World" and "Stop Killing Whales". Van Assche's venue featured Poem Paintings by artist John Giorno, who stencilled giant Hamnett-style slogans on the concrete walls.

Show
Menswear
Autumn/Winter
2013–14

Time/Date
18th January 2013
2pm

Place
Palais de Tokyo
13 avenue du Président-Wilson
Paris

Format/Size
Poster
84cm x 58.5cm
(33in x 23in)

Givenchy

In 2005, a decade after the label's namesake Hubert de Givenchy had retired and following in the footsteps of three British heavyweights – John Galliano, Alexander McQueen and Julien Macdonald, the young Italian Riccardo Tisci came to the brand as a relative unknown. From his debut installation-style presentation, the graduate of Central Saint Martins brought a poetic sense of melodrama and mystery to the house. For this show, inspired by his seaport home of Taranto, Tisci retold a folklore tale of sailors transforming into mermaids (the seabed silhouette featured on his invitation). That meant atmospheric staging featuring a behind-the-scenes tableau (the venue housed scenery and props for The Odeon theatre), dramatically spot-lit through a thick mist that hung heavily on the concrete floor. Models paraded serenely, seemingly unconcerned that they were trailing the trains of their gowns through the puddles. Men's uniform jackets were torn apart and stitched onto floaty chiffon dresses, with stiffened fishtail hems and theatrical fin collars.

Show
Haute Couture
Spring/Summer
2007

Date/Time
23rd January 2007
7.30pm

Place
Ateliers Berthier
32 boulevard Berthier
Paris

Format/Size
Double-sided poster
65cm x 49.5cm
(25½in x 19½in)

Alexander McQueen

Alexander McQueen was a designer who could not disconnect the process of designing from the opportunity for commentary, often causing him to become the target of criticism from naysayers who wanted no more than a retail experience from a catwalk show. McQueen had other ideas.

For this presentation, called "The Horn of Plenty", he turned his attention to the fashion industry's insatiable appetite for newness. The show was vintage McQueen, from the shattered glass catwalk and set (a giant scrapheap of fixtures and fittings from previous McQueen shows) to the exaggerated make-up that made models look like blow-up rubber sex dolls, further enhanced by plastic bags worn as hats, as seen on the invitation featuring a portrait by Hendrik Kerstens. And, of course, there were the clothes, which showcased the designer's impeccable tailoring skills. Giant houndstooth check was cut into updates of 1950s haute couture and his own sartorial greatest hits. For a series of finale gowns the houndstooth morphed into a flock of birds.

Ph. Hendrik Kerstens - Bag, 2007 · Courtesy Witzenhausen Gallery Amsterdam / New York

ALEXANDER
M(Q)UEEN

Autumn / Winter 2009
Tuesday March 10th 2009 8.00pm
Palais Omnisport Paris Bercy
8 Boulevard de Bercy
Salle Marcel Cerdan, Porte 28
Paris 75012

Drop off point Rue De Bercy

Press Contacts
Janet Fischgrund / Peitz Narmuliex
c/o KCD Paris T +33 1 40 96 20 76

Strictly non-transferable
Please bring invitation for admission

Show
Autumn/Winter
2009–10

Date/Time
10th March 2009
8pm

Place
Palais Omnisport de Paris-Bercy
8 boulevard de Bercy
Paris

Format/Size
Double-sided poster
59cm x 42cm
(23¼in x 16½in)

THE MAN WHO KNEW TOO MUCH

Alexander McQueen

Show
Autumn/Winter 2005–6

Time/Date
4th March 2005
8pm

Place
Lycée Carnot
145 boulevard
Malesherbes
Paris

Format/Size
Poster
83cm x 59cm
(32¾in x 23¼in)

McQueen gave this show the title "The Man Who Knew Too Much", a direct steal of the 1965 movie by Alfred Hitchcock, and presented the invitation as a reworking of the poster for *Vertigo*. McQueen was an admirer of Hitchcock's dark sensibility and storytelling and drew inspiration from his penchant for icy-cool leading ladies. In this show, which featured sleek wool suits, Sweater Girl knits, fur coats and lavish fishtail gowns, models (including Amber Valletta, Karen Elson and Carmen Kass) were coiffed by hairdresser Guido Palau into haughty Hitchcock heroines. The models were picked out by a sinister spotlight as they traversed a mezzanine walkway and staircase before parading in the gigantic auditorium against a backdrop straight out of *Rear Window*. The atmosphere was so chilly (perhaps part of McQueen's intention) that the invited guests were furnished with plaid lambswool blankets similar to fabrics featured in the collection. These became impromptu gifts.

Yohji Yamamoto

This show was presented in Yamamoto's Parisian headquarters, with models meandering their way through a maze of seated guests and concrete pillars. The atmosphere was hauntingly melancholic, both chilly and chilled – the first four models, swathed in shawls and blankets, emerged to the strains of José González's acoustic version of Massive Attack's "Teardrop". At the end of the show, these same blankets were transformed into coats outlined with colourful contrast stitching.

At times, Yamamoto's looks verged on the historical. The designer reworked formal frock coats, military jackets and tailcoats, adding scarves rakishly knotted into dandyish bows. The idiosyncratic casting for which Yamamoto is well known offered models of every shape, race, age and size. Many resembled reluctant heroes from an epic novel by Tolstoy. Comfort and protection seemed to be a theme, with a bulky tweed coat worn over what appeared to be satin pyjamas. The uniform overtones were emphasized with rows of gold buttons and woven regimental badges.

Show
Menswear
Autumn/Winter
2012–13

Date/Time
19th January 2012
6pm

Place
155 rue Saint-Martin
Paris

Format/Size
Poster
68cm x 44.5cm
(26¾in x 17½in)

MAN

This London menswear collective show offers an opportunity for new talents to present their work to the fashion industry without the expense of staging a solo venture. Masterminded by Lulu Kennedy (who also dreamed up Fashion East, its womenswear sister initiative) and sponsored by Topman, the MAN organization, which was set up in 2005, also provides mentoring for the young designers. Along with catwalk collections by Carola Euler, Siv Stoldal and Topman Design, there was also a film by Cassette Playa, the label of Carri Munden, and an installation by Aitor Throup, whose sketch appeared on the invitation. This was a breakthrough moment for Throup, who had earned rave reviews with his Royal College of Art graduation collection and was gathering something of a cult following. Throup is a conceptual designer who employs drawing and sculpture to inform his design process, so he took the opportunity to stage a, static presentation that was as much an art installation as a fashion parade.

Show
Menswear
Autumn/Winter
2007–8

Date/Time
16th February 2007
5.30pm

Place
The Old Sorting Office
21–31 New Oxford Street
London

Format/Size
Poster
59cm x 42cm
(23¼in x 16½in)

Marina Yee

Having studied at Antwerp's Royal Academy of Fine Arts, Marina Yee was one of the original Antwerp Six designers who travelled to London in 1986 to great acclaim. The group, part of a revolution sweeping through fashion and inspired by cultural movements such as punk and New Romantic, were described by *The New York Times* as bringing a "breath of inventiveness" to the London trade show. Marie was the name of her commercial collection. The mood of her designs was described as "dark and brooding", but, as the invitation suggests, they were deeply romantic with subtle detailing. At odds with what she felt was the "mindless commercialism" that gripped fashion, Yee disappeared from the scene at the height of the Antwerp Six's success. For a long time, she was often overshadowed by her classmates, who went on to build international brands, although she has since collaborated with Dirk Bikkembergs. She now reconstructs second-hand clothes into unique ensembles. Her work is deliberately low-key.

Show
Autumn/Winter
1987–88

Date/Time
14th–17th March 1987

Place
British Designer Show
Olympia 2
Hammersmith Road
London

Format/Size
Tinted acetate
32cm x 24cm
(13in x 9½in)

Show
Autumn/Winter
2002–3

Date/Time
13th February 2002
8pm

Place
Mercedes-Benz
Fashion Week
Bryant Park
West 42nd Street and
Broadway
New York

Format/Size
Holographic postcard
14.5cm x 10.5cm
(5½in x 4in)

Matthew Williamson

The 3-D image of colourful roses reiterated the mood of the show, while the title of the collection, "Kaleidescape", summed up the designer's aspiration – Matthew Williamson was intent on fashioning his own landscape as crazy and colourful as the world of Willy Wonka but inhabited by his supermodel friends, who included Carmen Kass, Liberty Ross, Elizabeth Jagger and Eva Herzigova. From his first collection, it was obvious that Williamson loves colour but by this showing in New York (his first on the American schedule) he had started to intensify his use of pattern and texture and had also begun to reimagine his vision of a modern wardrobe. This meant that while some outfits (coloured peach, pink, tangerine, mauve, turquoise and lemon offset with khaki) featured ethnic paisleys and tapestry-style blooms, others were decorated with sewn-on military badges and patches. Both were embellished with metallic lace and crystal embroideries lest the front row didn't get his mindset: enough is never enough.

Valentino

The show at the Grand Hotel, Paris, opened with Naomi Campbell, picked out against a sumptuous quilted backdrop in a shaft of light, wearing a long satin gown decorated with lilac orchids akin to the one featured on the invitation. She was accessorized with a naked man. Then the lights went out, they were gone and in their place was the Canadian model and actress Shalom Harlow in a neat red wool suit that was part Jackie O (one of Valentino Garavani's most celebrated clients), part Japan. The theme continued throughout this stellar Valentino couture show, with supermodels including Karen Mulder, Nadja Auermann, Kristen McMenamy, Carla Bruni, Claudia Schiffer and Campbell looking particular chic in abbreviated pastel suits, black-beaded lace and feathered dresses and golden satin ensembles that all referenced the Orient. Auermann modelled a black pagoda-shaped coat that she flamboyantly opened to reveal more orchids.

Show
Haute Couture
Autumn/Winter
1995–96

Date/Time
9th July 1995
7.30pm

Place
Salon Opera
Le Grand Hotel
2 rue Scribe
Paris

Format/Size
Card
19cm x 14cm
(7½in x 5½in)

KAREN WALKER AUTUMN/WINTER 2005/06

Karen Walker

Show
Autumn/Winter
2005–06

Date/Time
13th February 2005
8pm

Place
On/Off, Royal
Academy of Arts
6 Burlington Gardens
London

Format/Size
Card
21cm x 15cm
(8¼in x 5¾in)

Karen Walker is a New Zealander, who staged her debut solo show in London in 2002 and quickly established a cult following for her tomboy styles. In keeping with the designer's trademark of contrasting themes (masculine and feminine, luxury and casual, sleek and street), Ms Walker's "Tree Girl" muse for this season was an outdoorsy type, opting for a waterproof cape or a lush sheepskin jacket, along with cute velvet party dresses. She favoured striped reworked rugby shirts and silky ruffle-front dress shirts. One presumes that the rather sad young woman featured on the invitation is the "Tree Girl" from the collection's title. Certainly the catwalk palette was derived from this illustration, as were several prints. On the catwalk, the mood was decidedly chilly, with models, who included Theodora Richards (daughter of Rolling Stone Keith), wearing T-shirts layered under their little dresses and camisoles, while Ms Walker herself appeared at the end of the show to take her bow, snuggled in a woollen muffler.

Topman Design

Although the invitation offered a graphic flower design that featured on a collarless shirt worn by the first model in the show, the actual floral content in this collection was relatively low – just a few Liberty-style buds and one Warhol-esque cartoon bloom, both coloured mauve, red and yellow. Shirts were mostly a patchwork of cravat-style polka dots or printed with a running fox that also appeared knitted into sweaters. The presence of musicians Olly Murs and Labyrinth on the front row may have inspired the design team at Topman to add another motif: a spinning vinyl record.

A secondary theme in the collection involved utilitarian workwear. Trousers and shorts featuring multizip pockets and giant eyelets were held up with tough tan leather belts, while parkas worn over single-breasted suits added a casual look. Fabrics included hardy cotton drill, oilcloth, towelling, sweatshirting and wrinkled glazed cotton. The models carried tool kit bags covered in tiny metal badges.

Show
Menswear
Spring/Summer
2011

Date/Time
22nd September 2010
9.45am

Place
Royal Opera House
Covent Garden
London

Format/Size
Card
21cm x 21cm
(8¼in x 8¼in)

CONTRE LE SIDA

Soirée organisée
par les
couturiers et créateurs
de mode

LE MERCREDI 26 OCTOBRE 1988

Au profit des associations LE CERCLE DES MÉDECINS et ARCAT-SIDA.

Show
Charity gala

Date/Time
26th October 1988
7.30 pm

Place
Cour Carrée du Louvre
rue de Rivoli
Paris

Format/Size
Card
22cm x 15cm
(8½in x 6in)

Contre le SIDA

This gala dinner was the first large-scale benefit sponsored by the French establishment that directly addressed the devastating effect that AIDS (known in France as SIDA) was having on the fashion industry. The event, held in the fashion show tents at the Louvre at the tail end of the Spring/Summer 1989 Paris Fashion Week, was patronized by high-profile French politicians Jack Lang and Frédéric Mitterrand, and Pierre Bergé (Yves Saint Laurent's business partner). The 800 guests boasted big-name designers, including Karl Lagerfeld, Claude Montana, Thierry Mugler, Jean Paul Gaultier, Sonia Rykiel, Patrick Kelly, Kenzo Takada and Christian Lacroix, along with Marisa Berenson, Grace Jones, Jeanne Moreau and Jacqueline de Ribes. The evening included an upmarket raffle, a recital by Italian pianist Maria Tipo, and an auction that featured a unique quilt patchworked together by 36 designers. The image on the invitation, illustrated by René Gruau, was intended to represent love, pain, life and suffering.

Yves Saint Laurent

It was the end of an era when Yves Saint Laurent closed the doors of his couture house for ever. This show caused the centre of Paris to come to a standstill as the streets around the Pompidou Centre were gridlocked with bumper-to-bumper limousines chauffeuring guests unable to get through the crowds that surrounded the building, waiting to watch the show on giant screens outside. This retrospective was a tour de force trip through Saint Laurent's greatest sartorial hits, from the utilitarian safari jacket and pea coat to exotic eveningwear. There were looks inspired by Mondrian, Matisse, van Gogh, Picasso and Cocteau, along with others that referenced his love of travel: Africa, China, Russia and Spain. The finale, featuring an almost endless line-up of supermodels including Jerry Hall, Katoucha Niane and Carla Bruni wearing "Le Smoking" tuxedo looks, ended with the designer's appearance flanked by Catherine Deneuve and Laetitia Casta. The invitation features the jewelled heart that always made an appearance in his haute couture shows.

Show
Retrospective show
1962–1992

Date/Time
22nd January 2002
7pm

Place
Centre Georges Pompidou
19 rue Beaubourg
Paris

Format/Size
Card
20cm x 15cm
(8 x 6in)
Card (jewelled heart)
21cm x 15cm
(8¼ x 6in)

Acne

In 1996, Jonny Johansson established Acne in Sweden as a creative collective. Alongside the clothing label (Acne Studios), the brand also includes animation, design, advertising and even a magazine called Acne Paper, which has included contributions from the great and the good of the fashion industry, among them photographer Paolo Roversi, Carine Roitfeld, former editor-in-chief of French *Vogue*, and actress Tilda Swinton. The universal ethos of the label promotes a simple, functional fashion statement inspired by individuality.

In this show that meant furry jackets, leather trousers, quilted satin pieces with conventional suiting and cropped jackets over single-breasted blazers. Fluffy mohair sweaters and cardigans formed an approximation of a twinset. Odd styling details included wide shorts worn over narrow trousers and a baseball cap teamed with a tuxedo. Throughout, models wore white socks (previously seen as a fashion faux pas) and carried large leather or fur tote bags and matching gloves. Versions of the heart print featured on the invitation were used on shirts and trousers.

Show
Menswear
Autumn/Winter
2012–13

Date/Time
22nd January 2012
8pm

Place
165 rue de Vaugirard
Paris

Format/Size
Card
14cm x 20cm
(5½in x 8in)

Show
Autumn/Winter
1997–98

Date/Time
25th February 1997
8.30pm

Place
The Roundhouse
Chalk Farm Road
Camden Town
London

Format/Size
Card
4.5cm x 10.5cm
(1¾in x 4in)

Antonio Berardi

This show confirmed that Antonio Berardi was hot property. The designer had bagged himself an Italian backer, providing the opportunity to stage a big-production show at the cavernous music venue. The tiny folded invitation offered no indication of the scale of the presentation, although having once been an assistant of John Galliano perhaps it was not surprising that Berardi should ramp up the theatrics.

From behind canvas curtains a red glow emanated (possibly Hades?), while smoky fires burned around the perimeter of the circular metal-clad catwalk that threatened to topple the Manolo Blahnik-shod models. Looking war-weary, they emerged to a throbbing beat. First, Berardi's muse Michele Hicks, then Naomi Campbell; later, a regal-looking Honor Fraser cinched into a rib-crushing corset. In among the theatrics, Berardi's signature looks shone: the chiffon bias-cut dress with asymmetric hem, the exquisite frock coat now given a US cavalry twist, a skinny trouser suit or leather jacket inset with flames. Hicks closed the show in a nude tulle gown embroidered with flowers and a headdress ablaze with candles.

Nikos

Greek designer Nikos Apostolopoulos is best known for his somewhat racy underwear designs. His shows are loaded with theatricality, employing an endless variety of themes and tableaux vivants in each one. Over the seasons these have included Gatsby look-alikes, Arthurian knights and goddesses of both the silent screen and classical Greek varieties. For his Spring/Summer 1987 show against a backdrop of Romanesque columns a model made his entrance carrying a flaming torch astride a white stallion.

This collection was big on outerwear, with padded parkas and puffed jean jackets worn with Demob suits or studded leather and chainmail jeans. There were soigné velvet dressing gowns, satin pyjamas and even some see-through underpants. The finale was a glittering affair, with the model in the silver sequin suit trying to out-sparkle the guy in a gold leather puffa jacket and matching jeans sporting a pair of gold wings, just like the illustration by James Dignan on the invitation.

Show
Menswear
Autumn/Winter
1990–91

Date/Time
3rd February 1990
6.30pm

Place
Pavillon Gabriel
5 avenue Gabriel
Paris

Format/Size
Card
21cm x 15cm
(8¼in x 6in)

Show
Spring/Summer
2003

Date/Time
15th September 2002
7.30pm

Place
Stationers' Hall
Ava Maria Lane
London

Format/Size
Paper
10.5cm x 13cm
(4in x 5in)

Eley Kishimoto

Mark Eley and Wakako Kishimoto formed their partnership in the early 1990s, working on textile collaborations with designers including Marc Jacobs and Jil Sander. The use of pattern and print has become part of the label's identity. Their aesthetic rejects trends and fads. The naive, illustrated invitation, printed on cartridge paper that could have been torn from a sketchbook, emphasizes their handcrafted, organic approach. The homely scene – the cat, the curtains and the overflowing fruit bowl – is another hint at the duo's nostalgic yearning for a simpler life.

The venue for the show, the Stationers' Hall, is one of London's most fabulous historic buildings. For the show the pair added "EK" flags among the theatrical stained-glass windows and heraldic shields. Before the show began Elizabethan music was played at full volume. The models, who walked directly on the wooden floor, wore tomboy work shirts (with matching ties), tapestry knee-length skirts, dungarees, sun-tops and, of course, cute, jazzy print frocks.

Bella Freud

It is not every designer who had a celebrated artist such as Lucian Freud for a father, who might scribble off a logo for you over breakfast, but that is the apocryphal tale that surrounds Bella Freud and the illustration of her whippet, Pluto. Freud launched her label in 1990 and unsurprisingly, given the designer's unconventional upbringing, her designs err on the quirky – old-school tailoring and charm-school dresses are interspersed with too-cool-for-school sweaters bearing cartoon drawings (including that dog) and enigmatic bon mots. These have become a favourite with Freud's style-icon friends such as Kate Moss and Alexa Chung. Throughout her career the designer has used a variety of media from film (co-directing with filmmakers James Lebon and John Malkovich, among others) to a magazine edited with Sixties icon Anita Pallenberg.

    Freud, who exudes the same kind of charismatic English eccentricity as her one-time boss, Vivienne Westwood, has gone on to collaborate with exceedingly British brands Biba, Miss Selfridge, Barbour and Jaeger.

Show
Spring/Summer
1992

Date/Time
11th–14th October 1991

Place
The London Designer Show
Duke of York's Headquarters
King's Road
London

Format/Size
Card
15cm x 21cm
(6in x 8¼in)

Modern Classics

Show
Promotional material

Date/Time
1980

Place
71 Rivington Street
Shoreditch
London

Format/Size
Card
10.5cm x 15cm
(4in x 6in)

Willie Brown is a designer who emerged from the New Romantic milieu, dressing pin-ups Spandau Ballet and Steve Strange. Brown's clothes were his idea of a future world, as seen through the eyes of Bauhaus and Russian Constructivism. Minimal embellishment was offered and he used press-studs to fasten necklines, cuffs and waistbands. His fabrics, including cotton drill, were hardy, his colours muted – grey, navy, forest green and chestnut were favourites. Brown's muse was Vivienne Lynn (now Vivienne Tribbeck), a china-doll model who later became a fashion editor. Lynn was the perfect advertisement for the brand, wearing the designs as she worked in Brown's tiny store, Modern Classics.

At this time, East London was still a wilderness, so Modern Classics became a destination store for those in the know. The opening times were typed on the back of this card; the store was closed Monday and Tuesday. Brown staged a fashion show called "Clothes For A Temperate Isle" at the Blitz nightclub in March 1980. He now fronts the label Old Town, based in Norfolk.

Hermès

The luxury house of Hermès, established in 1837, originally began as a harness workshop (the logo is a horse and carriage), so it was appropriate that for this season's catwalk show in Paris, designed by then incumbent designer Jean Paul Gaultier, models were accompanied by a soundtrack featuring galloping horses. Wearing riding hats and with faces shrouded in net veiling, the models wore capes, sheepskin and fur shrugs, chunky-knit sweaters, glittery lace and brocade evening ensembles and chiffon scarves.

The equestrian theme translated into the accessory collection, shown in London, and included a silk twill scarf featuring a black-and-white illustration of a horse similar to the one on the invitation, long leather gloves, enamel bracelets featuring a horse-drawn coach, and silver and calfskin hairbrushes that resembled authentic grooming kit. Today, the Hermès customer can treat his/her horse to an exquisite leather saddle, leg bandages (in the house's signature shade of orange) or crocheted cotton ear-nets.

Show
Accessories
Autumn/Winter
2006–7

Date/Time
20th April 2006
10am–6.30pm

Place
Gallery 27
27 Cork Street
London

Format/Size
Paper
42cm x 30cm
(16½in x 11¾in)

JOHN GALLIANO
at the
BRITISH DESIGNER SHOW
OLYMPIA 2 LONDON W.14
OCTOBER 13th–16th 1984

SPRING–SUMMER '85
AFGHANISTAN
REPUDIATES WESTERN IDEALS

BUYERS CONTACT 247-4063. PR CONTACT JEAN BENNETT 405-5598

John Galliano

Following his famous graduation fashion show at Central Saint Martins John Galliano left it a year or so before he took to the catwalk again. Instead he showed his collection to press and buyers on a static stand during London Fashion Week at the British Designer Show. Galliano has said that, inspired by the old cartoon from *Punch* magazine that features on the invitation, he researched King Amanullah, who, following a trip to England, was so impressed by Western style that he tried to impose Savile Row on his subjects. For his collection the designer mixed bankers' pinstripes with Afghani tunics, twisted tailoring and Islamic woven fabrics in exquisite berry colours. Voluminous zouave pants were held up with braces – "It had a Brick Lane vibe to it," said Galliano. This anarchic edge and subversive spirit also showed in the accessories: broken spectacles. It was with this collection that Galliano began to collaborate with *Harpers & Queen* (now *Harper's Bazaar*) fashion editor Amanda Grieve, now Harlech.

Show
Spring/Summer
1985

Date/Time
13th–16th October 1984

Place
British Designer Show
Olympia 2
Hammersmith Road
London

Format/Size
Card
23.5cm x 15.5cm
(9¼in x 6¼in)

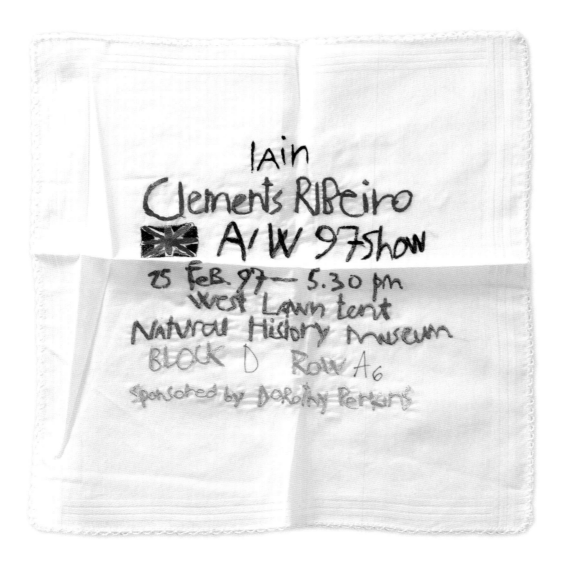

Iain
Clements Ribeiro
A/W 97 show
25 Feb. 97 — 5.30 pm
West Lawn tent
Natural History Museum
BLOCK D Row A6
Sponsored by Dorothy Perkins

Clements Ribeiro

It is perhaps not surprising that Clements Ribeiro's hankerchief invitation with the name of each guest individually embroidered on it became the season's most coveted accessory at London Fashion Week. The Union Jack highlighted how husband-and-wife team Suzanne Clements and Ignacio Ribeiro liked to do a little flag waving themselves for British design and manufacturing. For this show they dressed Naomi Campbell in a red, white and blue Union Jack cashmere sweater (Kate Moss also modelled the design for a photo call) – both images were beamed around the world. For a cover of *Elle* UK magazine they dressed Campbell again, this time in a specially designed dress made out of a souvenir flag purchased from an Oxford Street vendor. The designers' inventiveness and homespun style made them perfect style ambassadors as part of "Cool Britannia", the 1990s pop culture version of patriotism. Their emblemic style continues to be a combination of couture craft (of which this invitation is perhaps a fine example) and effortless, urban cool.

Show
Autumn/Winter
1997–98

Date/Time
25th February 1997
5.30pm

Place
West Lawn Tent
Natural History Museum
London

Format/Size
Handkerchief
28.5cm x 27.5cm
(11¼in x 10¾in)

YOHJI YAMAMOTO
HOMME
PRINTEMPS-ETE
2012
JEUDI
23
JUIN
A 18:00

155, RUE SAINT-MARTIN
75005 PARIS
PRESSE TEL. +55 (0)1 42 78 94 11
FAX. +55 (0)1 42 78 87 59

Show
Menswear
Spring/Summer
2012

Date/Time
23rd June 2011
4pm

Place
155 rue Saint-Martin
Paris

Format/Size
Handkerchief
33.5cm x 34cm
(13¼in x13½in)

Yohji Yamamoto

Against the bare-bones backdrop of his showroom, Yamamoto showed loose, flapping oversized shirts, long roomy jackets and vast pleated over-trousers, which resembled skirts that were part culottes, part chaps. Although the collection was dominated by the designer's favoured monochrome palette (highlighted by the cotton handkerchief invitation), there was an extensive use of colour from subtle faded shades of pink and china blue to verdant greens and bold stabs of red. Military-style tailored jackets were teamed with swagged ethnic trousers and worn with tough boots or plimsolls. The soundtrack, compiled by Jiro Amimoto, was described by one critic as "peppy Asian pop", but Yamamoto's world is truly global – his models were an eclectic mix of European, Asian, African and Middle Eastern; youthful and aged, short and tall, pin thin or portly, smooth-skinned androgynous or Grizzly Adams hairy. Several wore Yamamoto's trademark trilby. The designer appeared at the end of the show in his own approximation of the look, trilby and all.

ANN DEMEULEMEESTER
(men)

2013 - 2014

VENDREDI 18 JANVIER 2013 A 11H00
ENSBA SALLE MELPOMÈNE 13 QUAI MALAQUAIS 75006 PARIS

PRESSE MICHÈLE MONTAGNE +33 1 42 03 91 00
press@michelemontagne.com

Ann Demeulemeester

Throughout her career, designer Ann Demeulemeester has never wavered from her aesthetic, an intriguing combination of romance and realism, darkness and optimism. For this show, the pragmatic tone of her invitation, a virginal handkerchief simply printed, was softened by a barely visible white-on-white print and a delicately pleated border. The designer used swathes of similar fine white cotton drapes as a wistful backdrop to this powerful monochrome collection.

   With a soundtrack featuring Nick Cave & The Bad Seeds performing "O Children", there was a sense of the spiritual in the air, not least because Demeulemeester's wan-faced models, in their white roll-neck oversized shirts layered with black waistcoats and elongated jackets, bowler hats and gaitered boots, resembled eighteenth-century clergymen. Several models wore funereal net veils, while others were accessorized with raven's feathers. In November 2013, Demeulemeester shocked the fashion world when she announced that she was leaving her label for "new challenges in life".

Show
Menswear
Autumn/Winter
2013–14

Date/Time
18th January 2013
11am

Place
Salle Melpomène, ENSBA
13 Quai Malaquais
Paris

Format/Size
Handkerchief
40cm x 40cm
(15¾in x 15¾in)

Show
Spring/Summer
2005

Date/Time
13th September 2004
2pm

Place
The Theater
Bryant Park
New York

Format/Size
Bandana
53cm x 54.5cm
(30in x 21½in)

Anna Sui

New Yorker Anna Sui is a big fan of Americana so it was no surprise, given the cotton bandana invitation, that this season the designer offered her version of Wild West style, from Laura Ingalls in *Little House on the Prairie* (a longtime favourite of Sui's) to David Cassidy and Elvis in their spangled stage gear via freaky rock fans at Woodstock. That meant broderie anglais cotton petticoats and pin-tucked camisoles (think Katharine Ross in *Butch Cassidy and the Sundance Kid*), faded folksy florals, soft chamois and denim lookalike Confederate uniforms. The styling reflected the theme with models, bedecked in silver and turquoise trinkets, wearing beat-up cowboy boots and Stetsons that looked like they had gone three rounds at the local rodeo. Against a painted prairie backdrop with a picture-perfect sunset, Sui played Cowboys and Indians, accessorizing Naomi Campbell's fringed finale dress with an authentic-looking Native American feather headdress.

Paul Smith

Paul Smith first showed his collections in Paris in 1976. The designer revelled in his Englishness; happy to export what the French called *"le style Anglais"*. He offered his versions of upper-crust British tailoring with nifty eccentric touches. A collision of traditional tweeds and denim, or a floral print inspired by an old seed packet turned his clothes into something unique. For Autumn/Winter 1989 Smith fashioned a duffle coat from an old blanket and offered rainbow coloured knitwear.

Having started his career as a shopkeeper, Smith understands his customer and his stores showcase his eclectic taste. Alongside a pinstripe suit he sells bicycles, china knick-knacks and a peach mushroom print T-shirt.

These charming illustrations harking back to yesteryear underline Smith's talent as an imagemaker, and the designer has cultivated this spirit of nostalgia. His choice of venue for these shows – the L'Automobile Club de France – is an institution rich in heritage, being the first automobile club in the world, founded in 1895.

Show
Menswear
Autumn/Winter 1989–90
Spring/Summer 1989

Date/Time
2nd February 1989, 7pm
1st September 1988, 7.30pm

Place
L'Automobile Club de France (ACF)
6 place de la Concorde
Paris

Format/Size
Handkerchief
42cm x 42cm
(16½in x 16½in)

Official Souvenir

I HAVE VISITED
THE HOUSE OF MR. & MRS.

Antoni & Alison

ESTABLISHED 1820

TEA TOWEL   400×615MM   MADE IN ENGLAND

Show
Spring/Summer
2006

Date/Time
21st September 2005
2.30pm

Place
80 Southwark Bridge
Road
London

Format/Size
Tea towel
50cm x 78cm
(19¾in x 30¾in)

Antoni & Alison

The invitation to view a collection of "New Restoration Works" referred directly to the renovation of their new HQ, a four-storey Georgian townhouse in London's Bermondsey. For the occasion the designers turned the tables on the fashion editors and buyers, who in an effort to see the designs on models located around the house were required to squeeze up staircases and navigate sideboards abundant with nick-nacks. As it was only possible to accommodate a certain amount of guests at any one time this was not to everyone's taste and one particular front row stalwart flounced off when told by a PR that he would have to wait for the next guided tour. Models posed tableau-style behind red ropes – one slept, one read a book, while another acted as scullery maid in the basement kitchen amid piles of crockery, sacks of potatoes and jam tarts (these were duly demolished by the assembled press). And on your way out, why not pick up an Official Souvenir Tea Towel?

John Galliano

The "I Heart Charlie" handkerchief, knotted at the corners, appeared a homage to the stereotypical Blackpool holidaymaker, but as the show began and model Scott Barnhill burst from a giant clock looking the spitting image of silent movie actor Charlie Chaplin, it was obvious that this collection was a homage to the "little tramp". White-faced doppelgangers marched in quick-time down the catwalk dressed in a variety of black-and-white shrunken jackets and baggy trousers, followed by a series of Buster Keatons, straw boater and all.

In hindsight, the obvious allusion to drugs ("Charlie" being the slang term for cocaine) was somewhat unfortunate given the tragic tale that unfolded in the spring of 2011. As the clothes featured in this show went on sale in stores, Galliano was arrested in Paris for an alleged anti-Semitic attack and was removed from both his eponymous label and his position as designer-in-chief at Dior.

Show
Menswear
Spring/Summer
2011

Date/Time
25th June 2010
8.30pm

Place
7 Place Vendôme
Paris

Format/Size
Handkerchief
26.5cm x 26.5cm
(10½in x 10½in)

'stephen burrows' world'

Show
Spring/Summer
2002

Stephen Burrows

Date/Time
11th February 2002
7–9pm

Place
Henri Bendel
712 Fifth Avenue
New York

Format/Size
Card
21cm x 21cm
(8½in x 8½in)

During New York Fashion Week press and buyers were invited to a cocktail party at Henri Bendel to celebrate "Stephen Burrows' World" at the famous New York department store, a stone's throw from The Plaza Hotel and Central Park. The African-American designer, who began his career in the 1960s, had originally opened SBW in Bendel's in 1970. This relaunch was hosted by André Leon Talley, *American Vogue*'s larger-than-life editor-at-large, who has been a longtime friend and supporter of the designer. The magazine dubbed this event "the party of the season". Burrows' forte is easy, sensual clothes cut from matte jersey in daring rainbow combinations, alluded to in the collage cut-outs featured on this invitation. This clever combination has earned him a faithful clientele that reads like a Who's Who of American glamour: Cher, Diana Ross, Lauren Bacall, Liza Minnelli, Jerry Hall and Barbra Streisand. His great friend and muse is model Pat Cleveland, who is the perfect advertisement for his designs.

MICHIKO KOSHINO

Michiko Koshino

At the beginning of the 1980s, London street style emerged as one of the most directional forces in the global fashion industry, with press, buyers (*and* designers) heading to the British capital just to stroll up and down King's Road or hang out in Soho in the hope of discovering the Next Big Thing. Several designers capitalized on the look of these urban trendsetters, including Michiko Koshino, Jean Paul Gaultier and Red or Dead. Koshino pioneered urban streetwear on her catwalk in fun-packed shows that managed to harness something of the scene's rebellious attitude in both presentation and styling, often featuring a cast of character models sourced directly from the street or found in nightclubs. Her collections focused on innovative design, such as the inflatable plastic clothes that she made her trademark. Japanese-born Koshino returned to the UK with a collection for Spring/Summer 2013 that referenced her 1980s roots.

Show
Spring/Summer
1986

Date/Time
12th October 1985
11.45am

Place
Duke of York Barracks
King's Road
London

Format/Size
Card
18cm x 28cm (open)
(7in x 11in)

Show
Book launch

Date/Time
20th September 2005
6.30–9pm

Place
Burberry
21–23 Bond Street
London

Format/Size
Card
14.5cm x 10.5cm
(5¾in x 4in)

Michael Roberts

This invitation was for the book launch of *The Snippy World of New Yorker Fashion Artist Michael Roberts*, by one of fashion's most loved, and feared, commentators. Roberts, who cut his teeth in the 1970s writing a sharp weekly column for *The Sunday Times* (previously he had assisted style icon Molly Parkin), is something of a Renaissance man. During his career, he has been a writer, stylist, photographer, filmmaker, painter and even designed rugs. This book featured his forté for paper cuts, lampooning the industry he so elegantly inhabits. Despite his withering one-liners and wicked caricatures, the one-time fashion director of *Tatler* and *Vanity Fair* maintains the respect of industry giants such as Karl Lagerfeld, who published this book, and Christopher Bailey, creative director for Burberry, who hosted the party at the label's flagship London store. During this season, Roberts would be further fêted with events at New York's Bergdorf Goodman and Tod's in Milan.

Kenzo

Guests arriving at the École des Beaux-Arts walked under fluttering paper chains fashioned from these delicate cut-out invitations (above). Gilles Rosier, then incumbent designer at Kenzo, took a trip to Mexico with designs featuring the same colours and lace detail. He layered pattern on pattern, with leafy jungle prints and floral embroideries juxtaposed alongside golden gaucho-style leather.

In 2004, Rosier was replaced by designer Antonio Marras. For his third collection for the label, Marras focused on lush pattern and texture. His muse was a bohemian beauty: part fairytale princess, part flowerchild. For the finale, the backdrop featuring giant blow-ups of the Arts and Crafts-inspired invitation (far right) revealed models posed in a tableau of a tumbledown mansion furnished with chandeliers, wicker chairs, fringed lampshades and oil paintings. The ultimate 1970s It Girl, veteran model Marisa Berenson, wore an embroidered sheepskin, patterned dress and giant bejewelled necklace. It was the perfect curtain call for a show, and label, dedicated to exotica.

Show
Spring/Summer
2003

Date/Time
6th October 2002
11am

Place
École des Beaux-Arts
14 rue Bonaparte
Paris

Format/Size
Tracing paper
14cm x 15cm
(5½in x 6in)

Show
Autumn/Winter
2005–6

Show
5th March 2005
1pm

Place
Carrousel du Louvre
Salle Le Nôtre
99 rue de Rivoli
Paris

Format/Size
Card
13.5cm x 15cm
(5½in x 6in)

Kenzo

Although the designer Kenzo Takada is Japanese by birth, his decision to relocate to Paris in the early 1970s defined the brand. An essential part of the Kenzo offer is its sense of fun so it is not surprising that incumbent designer Antonio Marras should turn to the godfather of French humour, Jacques Tati, for inspiration. The look featured all Tati's trademarks – half-mast trousers, trilby hat, umbrella and scarf. Marras added zany patterned sweaters, quirky animal-print gloves, shoes and matching valise, along with intellectual spectacles.

This show was staged in the original Kenzo store (opened in 1976 as Jungle Jap) on places des Victoires and for the finale the cast of models trooped outside, where they circled the famous mounted statue of Louis XIV in the centre of the square. They were joined by 20 or so classic Citroën DS cars (launched in 1955), directed by comedy gendarmes. The models were eventually whisked away on a Kenzo branded vintage bus.

Show
Menswear
Autumn/Winter
2010–11

Date/Time
23rd January 2010
11am

Place
3 place des Victoires
Paris

Format/Size
Wood
28 x 21cm
(11in x 8¼in)

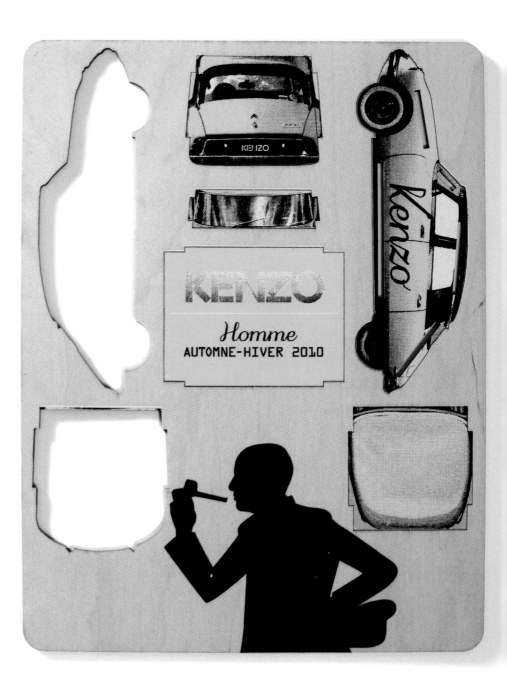

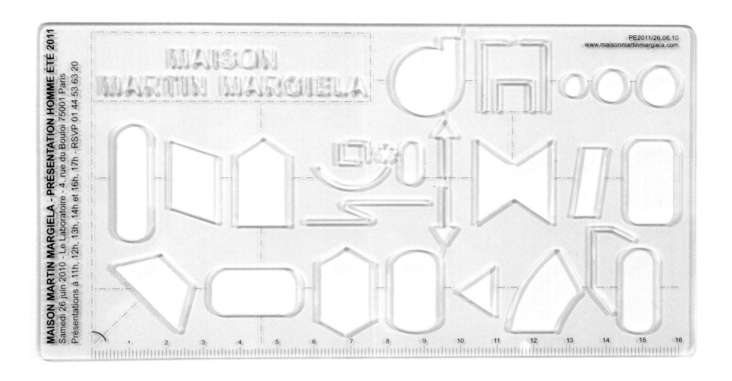

Show
Menswear
Spring/Summer
2011

Date/Time
26th June 2010
11am–5pm

Place
Le Laboratoire
4 rue de Bouloi
Paris

Format/Size
Plastic
9.5cm x 18cm
(3¾in x 7in)

Maison Martin Margiela

Maison Martin Margiela is known for its use of multimedia, so the backdrop for the day's presentations featured a projection of a short film of a photographic session documenting the collection. The film featured the labels instantly recognizable white-coated assistants, using white sheets and photographic stands to construct makeshift backdrops, which were then wheeled around various locations in the French capital. Not the glamorous picture-postcard Paris, but rather an anonymous park, a riverside pavement, a concrete high-rise estate and even the railings outside the Le Laboratoire show venue. During the shoot, models posed as the photographer dictated orders. MMM models are picked specifically for their individual looks and rarely fit the conventional ideal of a model.

The cut-out plastic invitation that resembles a chemistry-lab equipment template was appropriate as the presentations were staged at Le Laboratoire, an experimental space showcasing the fusion of art and science.

CFDA Foundation on behalf of the
Council of Fashion Designers of America
requests the pleasure of your company at
The 1994 CFDA Awards Gala

Monday, January 30, 1995

New York State Theater at Lincoln Center

RSVP card enclosed
black tie

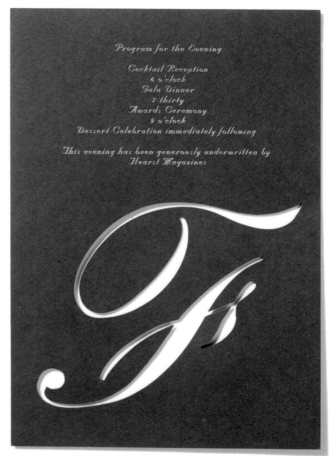

Program for the Evening

Cocktail Reception
6 o'clock
Gala Dinner
7 thirty
Awards Ceremony
9 o'clock
Dessert Celebration immediately following

This evening has been generously underwritten by
Hearst Magazines

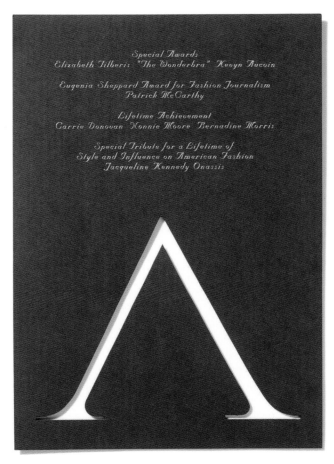

Show
CFDA Awards Gala
1994

Time/Date
30th January 1995
6pm

Place
New York State
Theater
Lincoln Center
New York

Format/Size
Card
19.5cm x 13cm
(7½in x 5¼in)

CFDA

The Americans love to applaud their own and nowhere is this more prevalent than in the fashion industry. the Council of Fashion Designers of America was organized in 1962 by publicist and philanthropist Eleanor Lambert with the aim of promoting home-grown talent on the global stage and to advance artistic and professional standards. Designer Diane von Furstenberg is the current president. The annual black-tie CFDA Awards have become synonymous with glamour, and A-list style icons such as Kate Moss, Anna Wintour and Sarah Jessica Parker are regulars on the red carpet. Winners at the 1994 event included Richard Tyler (Womenswear Designer of the Year) and Robert Lee Morris, whose sculptural jewellery for Donna Karan earned him the Accessories Award. *Harper's Bazaar* editor Elizabeth Tilberis and make-up artist Kevyn Aucoin were presented with Special Awards while Jacqueline Kennedy Onassis was feted with a Special Tribute. It doesn't get much more glamorous than that.

Pierre Balmain

At this time there was a revolution going on in Paris with designers such as Gianni Versace, Christian Lacroix and Karl Lagerfeld at Chanel determined to revitalize haute couture. New through the door at Balmain was New York-based designer Oscar de la Renta. Much was made of the fact that de la Renta was the first American since Mainbocher in the 1930s to head a French fashion house. The designer, who was tagged "the Sultan of Suave", was part of a new mood of reality chic emanating from Stateside. His aim was to make clothes women wanted to wear, not just showstoppers on the catwalk. He started by stripping away the packaging, presenting a confident and assured statement embodied by the simple "PB" initials. This was reflected in his refined and uncluttered style, as seen in the illustration by René Gruau, also featuring the matinée-idol handsome designer. The use of handwritten script alludes to an age of elegance and exclusivity befitting the customer of this label.

Show
Haute Couture
Autumn/Winter 1996–97

Date/Time
10th July 1996
2pm

Place
Grand Hotel
2 rue Scribe
Paris

Format/Size
Card
21cm x 15cm
(8¼in x 6in)

Show
Autumn/Winter
2005–6

Date/Time
4th March 2005
2.30pm

Place
Espace Ephémère
Grand Bassin de la
Concorde
Jardin des Tuileries
Paris

Format/Size
Card
11cm x 16cm
(9¼in x 6in)

Sonia Rykiel

Sonia Rykiel often decorates her designs with words and uses several different techniques to do this. Some are knitted, while others are highlighted in rhinestones. These words accentuate the mood or narrative of the collection. This show began in darkness with the designer's name picked out in crystal on the backdrop. Rykiel's fashion shows are always sparklingly optimistic in tone, with models parading in groups, arms linked, sharing a joke and/or flirting with the front row. This season they wore the designer's trademark black knits, decorated with twinkling rhinestones (the show's title featured on a sweater), stars and studs. Slouchy mannish pant suits were followed by lacy lingerie dresses, flowery frilled frocks and more knits twinkling with colourful Lurex thread. The soundtrack was an equally joyous mix, featuring Maroon 5, Alicia Keys and Charles Aznavour. And for the finale, a spotlit line-up of ruffled rainbow looks, led by model Lily Cole, sporting a crystal tiara spelling RYKIEL in her striking red hair. Totally Rykiel!

John Rocha

Hong Kong-born Irish designer John Rocha has always favoured fashion that celebrates artistic endeavour and craftsmanship. Many of his designs are one-offs and can take weeks of handwork to create. For his Paris debut Rocha teamed up with Irish artist Clea van der Grijn, encouraging the artist to paint freely on his fabrics. He then stitched up the results into garments for his show. Van der Grijn also designed the show programme and handcrafted over 300 invitations from pulped paper and chiffon embedded in the gold paint. She also created Rocha's three-moon logo and went on to create gigantic gold leaf installations for the Morrison Hotel in Dublin, the interiors of which were designed by Rocha.

   Taking its cue from van der Grijn's painted gold crosses, the collection had an ethereal theme with floaty, diaphanous fabrics and trailing hemlines, although the designer also added shots of pink, purple and red to the shimmering mix.

Show
Spring/Summer
1995

Date/Time
15th October 1994
4.30pm

Place
Carrousel du Louvre
Salle Gabriel
Paris

Format/Size
Handmade paper
24.5cm x 17cm
(9½in x 6½in)

Chanel

Show
Haute Couture
Autumn/Winter
1998–99

Date/Time
July 1998

Place
Chanel Boutique
31 rue Cambon
Paris

Format/Size
Booklet
29.5cm x 21cm
(11½in x 8¼in)

The burnished gold of the invitation and programme was carried through into the Chanel boutique at 31 rue Cambon, which was totally transformed when models walked through a maze of paper backdrops. These were roughly daubed with gold leaf. Even the famous mirrored staircase, where Coco herself once sat, was tipped with gold. The pared-back clothes, invariably long and ostentation-free, also gleamed with a whisper of glittery thread woven into the tweedy fabrics, while the models positively glowed, their scrubbed-clean faces illuminated with a shimmer of gold. Linda Evangelista, with a severe bobbed hairdo and wearing a pewter satin T-shirt dress, embodied easy elegance itself. With only a few accessories – a monastic-looking chain, disc brooch or a pair of flat sandals – Chanel designer Karl Lagerfeld cleverly offered a more casual way of dressing in haute couture that reflected the new laid-back mood in fashion. A vintage collection from the modernizer of fashion.

Sinha-Stanic

The unfussy gold bands encircling necks and waists perfectly defined the sleek and sophisticated aesthetic of designers Sinha-Stanic. Fiona Sinha and Aleksander Stanic, both in their mid-twenties at the time of this presentation, encapsulated the new breed of London designers offering a more grown-up, glamorous silhouette that incorporated a tough edge (the models were soundtracked by a trashing Garage band playing live). The pair also embodied New Britain's multiculturalism – she being half-Indian, half-Scottish, he born in Croatia. Having met at Central Saint Martins College of Art and Design in the late 1990s, they formed their label in 2004 when they became finalists in the Fashion Fringe design competition. Their designs have been worn by Beyoncé, Kate Moss and Pixie Geldof.

This collection's classic black and camel colour palette was enlivened with a shot of magenta and a shimmer of gold Swarovski crystals. A long, lean silhouette was achieved with cropped jackets, sky-high heels and even higher hemlines.

Show
Autumn/Winter
2006–7

Date/Time
17th February 2006
3.30pm

Place
20 Peter Street
London

Format/Size
Poster
42cm x 29cm
(16½in x 11½in)

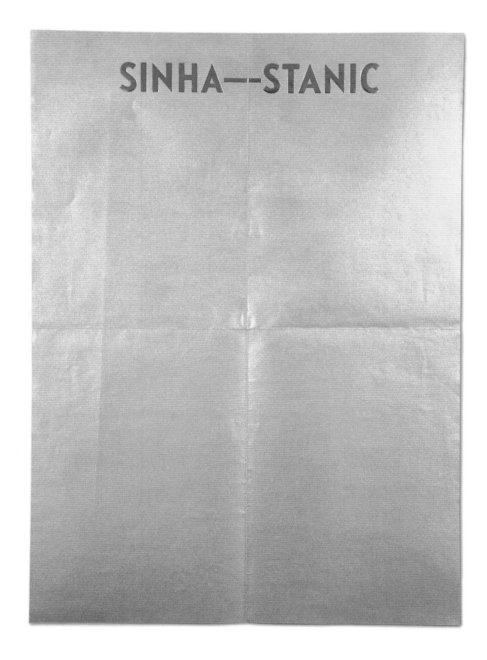

Show
Menswear
Spring/Summer
2013

Date/Time
28th June 2012
7pm

Place
165 rue de Vaugirard
Paris

Format/Size
Metal
3cm x 6cm
(1in x 2½in)

Dries Van Noten

Dries Van Noten's design ethos is a continual process, with one collection blossoming from another – except this time the designer replaced his trademark floral or ethnic prints with camouflage. Van Noten worked the military pattern in myriad different ways, emphasizing the mix in a sparse whitewashed warehouse space. While some outfits combined three different camouflage prints, the designer also added a dulled check and even lace. These were offset with navy blue and orange. With their slick side-parted hairstyles and strappy sandals, his models resembled fresh-faced GIs on shore leave (perhaps the stamped copper plate invitation alluded to a military dog tag?). They wore elegant jackets with Velcro fastenings, fencing-style tops, long shorts and ultra-fine knits. Van Noten's selection of fabrics was key – cotton voile and silk organza were quilted together to give a layered effect, yet the actual garments weighed next to nothing. Transparent nylon was printed with camouflage and cut into barely-there raincoats.

PIERRE et GILLES

Patrick Kelly

Shiny, camp, flamboyant and fun are not only words that describe this invitation featuring Patrick Kelly photographed by cult Parisian artists Pierre et Gilles, but also the designer's antics on the catwalk. In the 1980s the African American born in Mississippi became the first US member of the Chambre Syndicale du Prêt-à-Porter in France. Oft described as "exuberant" and "witty", nowhere was this more so than in this show, which featured an Americana theme of ponyskin and striped Navajo blankets alongside little black Lycra dresses accessorized with Native American headdresses. There were also dresses decorated with rhinestone versions of the Eiffel Tower worn with cycling caps (a Kelly trademark) that spelled out PARIS in crystal. Kelly loved colour and embellishment and many of his designs featured multicoloured buttons and bows. The humour often masked his sincere efforts to explore racial and social issues. Kelly's clothes made great photographs. He died on New Year's Day in 1990.

Show
Autumn/Winter
1989–99

Date/Time
15th March 1989
4pm

Place
Salle Perrault
Cour Carrée du Louvre
Paris

Format/Size
Card
21.5cm x 15.5cm
(8½in x 6¼in)

THOM BROWNE. NEW YORK Autumn / Winter 2012-13 Collection
Sunday 22 January 2012 6pm
Galérie de Minéralogie et de Géologie
Jardin des Plantes
36, rue Geoffrey Saint-Hilaire 75005 Paris

PR Consulting Paris / Nathalie Ours Tel. +33.1.73.54.19.51
tbrowne@kaleidoscopepr.net

Show
Menswear
Autumn/Winter
2012–13

Date/Time
22nd January 2012
6pm

Place
Galerie de Minéralogie
et de Géologie
Jardin des Plantes
36 rue Geoffrey Saint-
Hilaire
Paris

Format/Size
Card
9.5cm x 18.5cm
(3¾in x 7¼in)

Thom Browne

Browne's understated invitation did nothing to hint at his theatrical presentation.
In the futuristic French Communist Party HQ, designed by Oscar Niemeyer in the
1960s, journalists sat in the avant-garde domed auditorium set up for a press
conference. "We are excited on the return of our brave men," intoned a delegate
speaker for Browne. "Please hold questions until the end." Enter a line-up of
astronauts wearing white spacesuits and shiny helmets. These were divested to
reveal identical-looking young men with gold-leafed lips that matched their scaled-
up, mirrored Aviator sunglasses. Each wore a suit featuring cropped sleeves and
knee-length shorts; jackets were outlined in black or decorated with sharks or
bows. A seersucker stripe and madras check were both made of muted sequins.
As the collection flew the flag for the US space programme, Browne offered lots
of red, white and blue. The show ended with David Bowie's "Space Oddity". One
small step for Thom Browne, one giant leap for menswear.

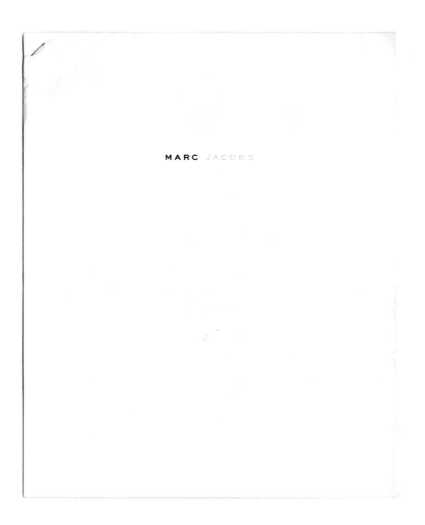

MARC JACOBS

Marc by Marc Jacobs

The previous evening designer Marc Jacobs had been trumpeting his mainline collection, quite literally. His show opened with the Nittany Lions Marching Band taking to the catwalk with a rousing rendition of Nirvana's "Smells Like Teen Spirit". There was even a baton-twirling bandleader in a glittering frock.

For his younger diffusion line show the mood was more raw and stripped-down, from the soundtrack compiled by Frederic Sanchez to the washed-out pastel palette. Jacobs filled his catwalk with the freshest-faced models, including Gemma Ward, Sasha Pivovarova, Toms Birkavs and Eugen Bauder, with minimal make-up and hair by Dick Page and Guido Palau respectively. The accompanying programme notes were presented in a similarly casual format: functional, low-cost photocopied sheets stapled together. Jacobs highlighted his Marc by Marc Jacobs collection by merely emphasizing his first name in bold type. Fittingly, the designer appeared at the end, accessorizing his grey suit with a pair of white sneakers.

Show
Spring/Summer 2006

Date/Time
12th September 2005

Place
Lexington Avenue
Armory
68 Lexington Avenue
New York

Format/Size
Paper
28cm x 21.5cm
(11in x 8½in)

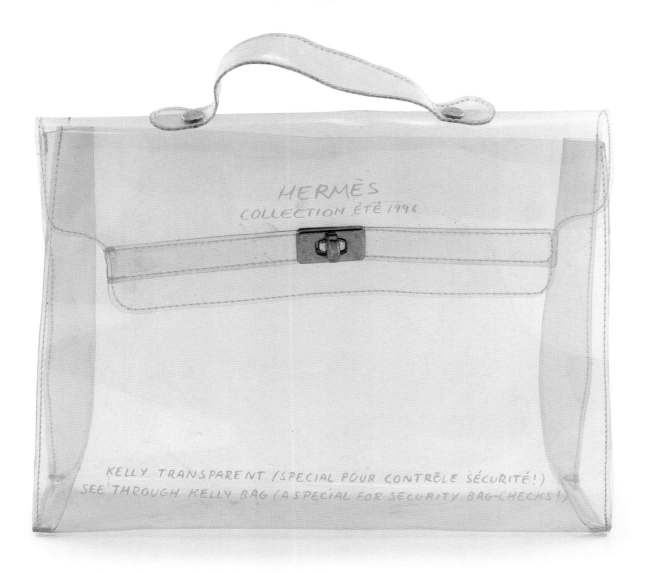

HERMÈS
COLLECTION ÉTÉ 1996

KELLY TRANSPARENT (SPECIAL POUR CONTRÔLE SÉCURITÉ!)
SEE THROUGH KELLY BAG (A SPECIAL FOR SECURITY BAG-CHECKS!)

Hermès

Show
Spring/Summer 1996

Date/Time
October 1995

Place
Carrousel du Louvre
99 rue de Rivoli
Paris

Format/Size
Plastic "Kelly" bag
25.5cm x 31.5cm
(10in x 12½in)

A fashion collection and surrounding promotional material can be influenced by cultural, social and even political events. During the summer of 1995 a spate of fatal bombing attacks on the French capital brought terrorism to Paris. A direct outcome was the heightened security surrounding the Spring/Summer 1996 shows, especially those held in public locations such as the Carrousel du Louvre.

Hermès sent their invitation to select journalists in this clear plastic version of the label's iconic "Kelly" bag, printed with the words: "A SPECIAL FOR SECURITY BAG CHECKS". This bag became a coveted front row item, especially when model Amber Valletta opened the show, carrying the plastic Kelly with a smaller leather version inside. But there were no signs of stress in this cool, elegant collection embodied by the line-up of models including Georgina Grenville, Christina Kruse and Carolyn Murphy. The sheer theme returned after dark, with black, pearl grey and café-au-lait see-through shirts worn with wafting chiffon skirts.

PRADA HAS THE PLEASURE OF INVITING

Adrian Clark   Cb11

TO THE SPRING/SUMMER 2013 MENSWEAR SHOW
SUNDAY JUNE 24TH AT 6:00PM
VIA FOGAZZARO 36 MILANO
RSVP 02 541 921

PRADA

Prada

The Prada Foundation venue housing this show featured a white architectural set (mimicking the invite), which models speed-walked around, their path traced in light. For this collection, it appeared Miuccia Prada had got the Olympic bug. The menswear show, which included older models John Rawlinson and John Pearson, also featured women wearing identical designs, a concept that runs parallel to the unisex sporting world. Central to the collection was a thick stripe outlining vests, headbands, sandals and even the inside leg of trousers. This kind of go-faster stripe, now so familiar on tracksuits and trainers, is one of the most potent of modern graphics often referenced by designers.

  After the show the designer commented backstage, in another nod to Olympians, "The border is a timeless decoration from Ancient Greece onwards." Perhaps Mrs Prada had tired of fashion's over-indulged diet of more, more, more and so, like Rifat Ozbek before her, offered a wardrobe of pared-down, functional and essentially anonymous athletic looks.

Show
Menswear
Spring/Summer
2013

Date/Time
24th June 2012
6pm

Place
Via Fogazzaro, 36
Milan

Format/Size
3-D acetate
13cm x 19.5cm
(5in x 7¾in)

Jil Sander

The invitation said it all: plain, plain, plain. This collection was Jil Sander at her most pared back to basics – a navy pant, a black dress, a shell top or pea jacket. In Sander's world, a polo neck sweater is simply elongated to become a dress. As usual, the collection was presented in her regular location, a narrow corridor of a venue devoid of colour, with only a lighting gantry overhead for decoration. Her clothes echoed the mood, often bereft of any kind of visible fastenings. The designer kept things edgy with seams on the outside and by playing with proportion – an oversized coat or a trouser cropped above the ankle – but the overall feel was utilitarian, taking its lead from the functionality, uniformity and attention to detail in a man's wardrobe. At that moment the woman Sander proposed was ice-cool, smart and sophisticated, embodied by models Kirsty Hume, Cecilia Chancellor and Kirsten Owen.

JILSANDER

8th MARCH 1996, 10.00 A.M.
PALAZZO DELLE STELLINE
VIA DE TOGNI 4, MILAN

SHOWROOM-PRESS OFFICE
VIA DE TOGNI 4, MILAN
TEL. 02/48 02 28 34 / 35 / 36

Jaz P. Webb
THE TIMES

Aa52

Show
Autumn/Winter
1996–97

Date/Time
8th March 1996
10am

Place
Palazzo delle Stelline
Via de Togni, 4
Milan

Format/Size
Card
26cm x 13cm
(10in x 5in)

Rick Owens

The concrete catwalk, at ground level per usual for Owens, was pricked by several columns of bright white light, through which the models emerged. From the preponderance of pale and sheer fabrics to the casting of more fresh-faced, youthful mannequins, the designer appeared to be looking to lighten the mood of this collection, titled "Island". While he still included several full-length enveloping robes, for which he has become best known, for the main part his outfits were sleeker and shorter in proportion. The designer talked about a newfound geometry in his designs and this materialized as a handful of patterns featuring triangles, squares and oblongs patchworked together. The tonal colour bar that appeared on the invitation became a print on sleeveless T-shirts, both black and white. While Owens' wife and business partner Michelle sang a poem by Langston Hughes over the soundtrack, the finale featured the models walking shoulder to shoulder en masse, as if some kind of spiritual future world army.

Show
Menswear
Spring/Summer
2013

Date/Time
28th June 2012
12.30pm

Place
8 boulevard de Bercy
Paris

Format/Size
Card
10.5cm x 29.5cm
(4in x 11¾in)

Balenciaga

The image featured on the invitation, photographed by the ultra-hip duo Inez van Lamsweerde and Vinoodh Matadin, oddly featured as the backdrop for the previous season's advertising campaign. Yet this still-life arrangement identified designer Nicolas Ghesquiere's favoured palette for this latest Balenciaga collection: a nude beige, tomato red and a wash of white, with an added dash of dulled emerald and lots of black. Against a backdrop of cold paving stones Ghesquiere's new look Balenciaga was ever true to Cristóbal Balenciaga's original forté – a dramatic blend of austere architectural line with a sense of the historical and romantic. The scrubbed-faced model girls were a perfect mix of the quixotic and quirky, epitomized by Colette Pechekhonova, who starred in the advertising campaign. With no visible fastenings, the clothes looked as spartan as the venue. The obi-style belts securing a slashed or pleated dirndl skirt lended a vague Oriental feel. Ghesquiere added the extra kudos of street credibility, aka cool!

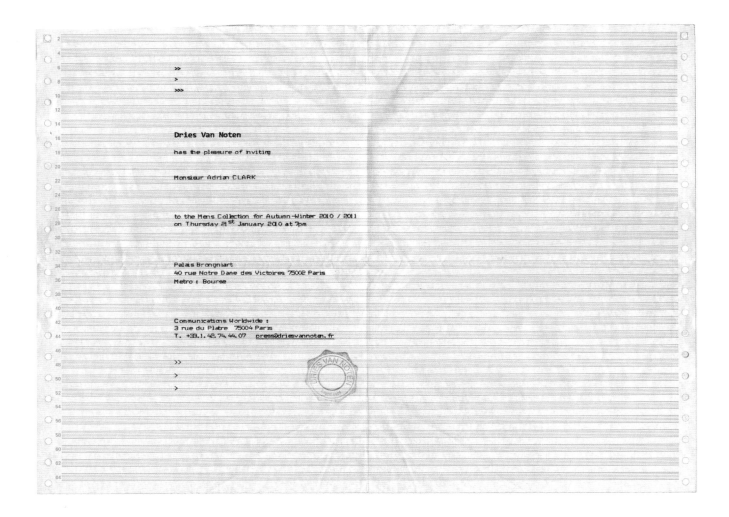

Dries Van Noten

Dries Van Noten's choice of the functional computer printout as his invitation heralded a no-fuss approach that ran through the collection and the presentation. Each model in the show carried a hand-held speaker, playing a mix of Moloko, The Clash, Snoop Dogg, Soft Cell and The Smiths. The effect was disorientating as the music ebbed and flowed among the building's classical columns. Perhaps this was Van Noten's aim, as the pragmatic designs he showed were equally unexpected, a discreet, no-nonsense statement bereft of the designer's signature clash of pattern and texture. This collection was all about the detail and fabric experimentation, which the audience got to examine up close as models paraded through narrow corridors inches away from the front row guests. However, Van Noten couldn't resist adding a few scholastic stripes, harking back to his earliest collections (again referencing the printout paper). This look was reinforced with collegiate scarves wrapped around the models' necks.

Show
Menswear
Autumn/Winter
2010–11

Date/Time
21st January 2010
7pm

Place
Palais Brongniart
40 rue Notre Dame des
Victoires
Paris

Format/Size
Computer printout paper
28cm x 38cm
(11in x 15in)

Calvin Klein
collection

section   B B

row   1

seat   8

Calvin Klein

Show
Calvin Klein Collection

Date/Time
circa 1992

Place
Milk Studios
450 West 15th Street
New York

Format/Size
Card
8.5cm x 12cm
(3½in x 4¾in)

With its stark interior, Milk Studios in New York City was the perfect setting for Calvin Klein's shows. From the early days, the designer favoured an uncomplicated, modernist style, earning him the title of King of Minimalism. Klein proposes a lifestyle that is synonymous with ultimate, effortless chic, embodied by the understatement and purity displayed in the super-simple graphics featured on this seat assignment card and his resolutely straightforward invitations.

In the early 1990s, when this card was used, Klein offered subtle, layered looks. Underwear was big business for the designer, so T-shirts, vests or slip-dresses were the basis of many outfits. Keen to be at the forefront of fashion, the designer embraced the new breed of individualistic, edgy-looking models such as Cecilia Chancellor, Debbie Deitering and Lucie de la Falaise, who walked alongside Klein's long-time favourite, Lauren Hutton.

Nothing in the world of Calvin Klein is overdone, be it an invitation to view his collections or a single Arum lily arranged artfully in a glass vase in his office.

Jain R. Webb 81

Ally Capellino

Although now perhaps better known for her bags, designer Alison Lloyd launched her first womenswear collection for Ally Capellino in 1980 and became an integral part of the alternative London fashion scene. As the white-on-white graphics of this invitation suggest, Lloyd favoured a quiet aesthetic combined with a fondness for the functional that ran through her collections. This show featured a muted palette dominated by an array of soft grey tones offset with pale blue. The designer offered a relatively uniform straight-up-and-down silhouette, playing instead with texture: fabrics included washed and slub silk, paper taffeta, matt cotton and shiny knit. The translucence of the trace paper invitation was hinted at with the inclusion of sheer fabrics. One model sported a folded paper hat.

In 1996 the designer also launched her "AO" range at London's Serpentine Gallery, sponsoring the Jean-Michel Basquiat exhibition. In 2006 she designed a range of bags for the Tate gallery and in 2010 celebrated her thirtieth anniversary with an exhibition at the Wapping Project that featured a "Wall of Bags". Along the way, the ever-practical Lloyd designed uniforms for the Girl Guide and Brownie associations.

Show
Spring/Summer
1996

Date/Time
21st October 1995
4.30pm

Place
BFC Tent
Natural History Museum
Cromwell Road
London

Format/Size
Acetate
23.5cm x 41cm
(9¼in x 16in)

JULIEN MACDONALD
AUTUMN WINTER 2013

VIVA LAS VEGAS

LUXOR
MGM
HAZE
BLACK JACK
MIRAGE
BELLAGIO
POKER
PONTOON
BACCARAT
FOUR SEASONS
COLLOSSEUM
NEVADA
STARTOSPHERE
MANDALAY BAY
SHIMMER
CASINO
VEGAS SUNRISE
CASINO ROYALE
GOLDEN SUNSET
LADY LUCK
SILVER NUGGET
BELLEZA
RAVELLA
RED ROCK CASINO
CAESARS PALACE
ARIA
RENAISSANCE
RUMOR
GREEN VALLEY
THE PLATINUM
VDARA
WESTIN
STARDUST
PALMS
VENETIAN
ROULETTE
PALAZZO
WYNN

Julien Macdonald

Everyone knows that Julien Macdonald loves glamour but this season the designer upped the glitz factor. The collection was called "Viva Las Vegas" and was inspired by a trip to the gambling capital, so it was not surprising that the sparkle never stopped coming. Where other designers might share their fabrics, silhouettes and colourways Macdonald chose to list casinos. But, after all, Macdonald's muse is a 24:7 attention-seeking party girl with messed-up hair and make-up who wears punky ankle boots with her evening gown.

The designer himself was in a flamboyant mood, showcasing the workmanship of his team, who embellished everything that moved with rhinestones, crystals, sequins and chains. A flashy lace and glitter bodysuit was reminiscent of Cher (a Vegas headliner), while the red finale number was pure tattooed, tasselled showgirl. One silver sequinned dress with sheer side panels became a favourite with performers Beyoncé and Ellie Goulding. Macdonald's front row, front-page guests were the girl group, The Saturdays.

Show
Autumn/Winter
2013–14

Date/Time
16th February 2013
3pm

Place
Goldsmiths' Hall
13 Foster Lane
London

Format/Size
Card
21cm x 15cm
(8¼in x 6in)

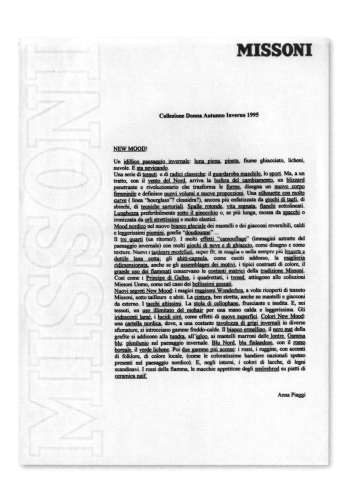

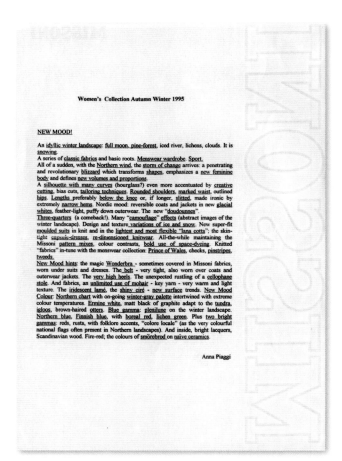

Missoni

Designers have wildly differing approaches to what they wish to offer their audience in the way of a backstory to the collection. While some present visual references and glossy promotional images that can be zapped straight to the news desk by headline-hungry fashion reporters, others prefer to limit their proposition to a few cryptic words. And then there are the designers who enjoy weaving a narrative among the seams. For this collection the flamboyant style icon Anna Piaggi, an editor at Italian *Vogue* and longtime friend of the Missoni family, was asked to pen words that were somewhere in the middle. Piaggi sets the scene: "An idyllic winter landscape ... it is snowing ... all of a sudden the storm of change arrives ..." This is followed by a description of the collection in terms of "revolutionary" silhouettes, colours, proportions and fabrics. Later, "the unexpected rustling of a cellophane stole". On the catwalk such fashion speak translates as Lurex knits, "snowball" polka dots, sparkly Missoni logos and quilted nylon ballgown skirts.

Show
Autumn/Winter
1995–96

Date/Time
March 1995

Place
The Fiera
Strada Statale del
Sempione, 28
Milan

Format/Size
Paper
29.5cm x 21cm
(11½in x 8¼in)

WOMAN.KNOTCH.SCULLY.WICKLOW.
CROCHET.VOLUME.BOWIE.FELT.GEORGE.
RUFUS.OLIVE.TEXTURE.AUTUMN.JAGUAR.
SALLY-GAP.CASHMERE.TUFT.FORM.SILK.
ZOE.MOHAIR.CIRCLES.PROPORTION.LEAF.
THIRTEEN.MAX.TIME.VILLAGERS.TAHITI.
TWO-THOUSAND.TRADITION.MO.HATS.
HANK.EMBELLISH.QUIRK.FRANCIS.SALMON.
JOHNROCHA.SCALE.BLACK.BODY.LACE.
DOUBLE JERSEY. LOVE. FIELDS. FLY. GREEN.
FRENCH KNOT.WINTER.VOLUME.COLOUR.
HAPPY. SKIN. HULME. FLOSS. HEATHER.
POSITIVE. PINK. STITCH. WAIST. GLOW.

Show
Autumn/Winter
2013

Date/Time
16th February 2013
2pm

Place
British Fashion Council
Catwalk Show Space
Somerset House
The Strand
London

Format/Size
Card
14.5cm x 21cm
(5¾in x 8¼in)

John Rocha

One very obvious way for a designer to share his inspirations is to spell them out to the audience and that's exactly what designer John Rocha did with the invitation for this collection. As soon as the invite arrived, his guests could see that fabrics such as felt, mohair, double jersey and lace were key; pink, olive and green formed his chosen colour palette; and Tahiti, David Bowie, Hank Williams, Wicklow and someone called Mo were all influences. Rocha also listed his music promoter son Max, who curated the soundtrack for the show.

The look was pure Rocha with bell-shaped dresses constructed from swirling petals of chiffon and circles of crochet, cape-like coats and jackets topped with wafting black tulle headdresses. Perhaps inspired by the success of his daughter Simone (although she wasn't listed), there was the addition of a new longer, slimmer silhouette featuring a slashed sleeve, which gave the collection a modern edge.

Band of Outsiders

The debate surrounding the purpose and effectiveness of a catwalk fashion show versus cost and production problems is a continuing conundrum for the industry. Each season there are designers who attempt to do something different in an effort to address the problem. For this menswear show LA-based Scott Sternberg decided to forgo the brouhaha surrounding the catwalk and instead create an art gallery installation-style presentation in the trendy Marais district of Paris with just one model. Sternberg then outlined his aims with a manifesto (a detail of which is shown here): the model would remain in a box constructed adjacent to the gallery's window for the duration of the show (60 hours in total), including sleeping. He could be viewed through the window and would change his outfit every 90 minutes, photographed standing by a digital clock.

The show was broadcast live on the label's website and shared via social media, thereby enabling the brand to reach a much larger audience than an invite-only guest list.

Show
Menswear
Spring/Summer
2013

Date/Time
29th June 2012
6.30–9.30pm

Place
Galerie Dominique Fiat
16 rue des Coutures Saint- Gervais
Paris

Format/Size
Poster
58cm x 44.5cm
(22¾in x 17½in)

These are the rules of the Show:

1. The Show will take place over sixty (60) hours, beginning on June 27th, 2012 at 09:30 and ending on June 29th, 2012 at 21:30.
2. There will be only one (1) Model in the Show.
3. The Show will take place inside a small compartment built from cardboard boxes and wood planks adjacent to the window of an anonymous gallery in Paris; the Model will be visible the entire duration through the window on the street.
4. The Model will only leave the compartment every ninety (90) minutes during waking hours (09:00 to 21:00) to have his photograph taken, to change into the next look from the collection as chosen by the Staff, to acquire a prop for the next section of the Show, and presumably to relieve himself every so often.
5. The Model will sleep in the compartment.
6. The Show will be broadcast live at the-longest-show-ever. bandofoutsiders.com and nowfashion.com for the entire sixty hours; photographs, music and supplemental information will be posted on the-longest-show-ever.bandofoutsiders.com and distributed through various "social media platforms" by the Staff throughout the three (3) days.
7. Throughout the duration, the Staff will create an archive of the presentation and exhibition of the collection inside the gallery. Materials they use will be limited to the following (or similar) items:
   a. A crappy, old photocopy machine.
   b. An electric typewriter.
   c. A Dymo machine (analog) and black tape.
   d. A time/stamp clock (aka an "Employee Time Clock").
   e. A rubber stamp, with Quotation icon.
   f. Artists Tape, various colors.
   g. Miscellaneous sticky, gluey substances.
   h. A Polaroid Land Camera, "The Reporter" Model.
   i. FUJI Black and White 3000 speed Pack Film.
   j. A digital camera, standard variety.
   k. Melamine clipboards, various sizes.
   l. Newsprint.
   m. Wooden Hangers.
   n. Twenty (20) 8" Security Monitors, various brands.
   o. Slide Projectors, (preferably Kodak Ektagraphic model iiiA or digital equivalent).
   p. Misc. wooden and metal stools and crates.
   q. Three (3) video cameras, for both broadcast and taped footage.
   r. The Spring 13 men's collection pieces.
8. Guests are encouraged to visit the window at any time throughout the duration of the Show, and can make appointments to preview the exhibition in progress through william@prconsultingparis.net (EU), johnk@framenoir.com (US), or iki@guthrie.co.jp (Japan).
9. Guests are also invited to view the exhibition (in progress but nearly complete) on Friday, June 29th between 18:30 and 21:30 when finally the Model will leave the window and the Show will end.

URBAN ROMANCE...SLEEK, POWERFUL, AND WOMANLY...
LEAN VS. LANGUID.....SEASONLESS CREPES AND
JERSEYS....SENSUAL SUEDES AND CASHMERES.... THE
GLOSS OF PYTHON.... THE SLINK OF MESH....LIQUID
SILKS.... THE SHOULDER REVEALED THROUGH SLIDING
NECKLINES, STRAPLESSNESS AND BARE CAMISOLES....
THE BACK EXPOSED THROUGH SENSUAL HALTERS...LEAN
TROUSERS, LEGGINGS, SKIRTS, UNITARDS, AND DRES-
SES FORM A BASE FOR MODERN DRESSING........THE
SOFTER SHIRT..... THE SHAPELY DINNER JACKET....
THE QUINTESSENTIAL LEAN COAT.... SHADES OF NUDE
AND SUNTAN BECOME NEW NEUTRALS...... THE IMPACT
OF BLACK..... THE CLARITY OF WHITE......GRAPHIC
SLASHES OF SCARLET... RICH SHADES OF BROWN FROM
KHAKI TO MAHOGANY........ GUNMETAL GREY, A NEW
OPTION FOR SPRING IN LIQUID SILK JERSEYS AND
CRISP SHARKSKIN..... THE PROVOCATIVE SLING BACK
SHOE... LANGUID MUFFLERS SOFTEN THE EDGE... THE
TAILORED CLUTCH BAG AND BELT...... UPSWEPT HAIR
AND A DRAMATIC EYE.... THE COMPONENTS TO FINISH
THE LOOK.... SPARE, LEAN, AND LUXURIOUS.... THE
TIMELESS ELEGANCE OF A DANCERS WARDROBE...
MOBILITY AND EASE ESSENTIAL FOR LIFE TODAY.....
SPRING '97 AT MICHAEL KORS

Michael Kors

American designers are renowned for their minimalist approach to fashion, with none more so inclined than Michael Kors. Originally he showed his collections in his own small showroom with just a handful of models. These intimate presentations enabled the editors and buyers to get a close look at the designer's work and appreciate the pared down luxury that has become his trademark. Although by this time showing in the cavernous tents at Bryant Park, Kors continued on a mission with his inspirational show notes listing "timeless elegance", "spare, lean, luxurious" and "mobility and ease essential for life today". That meant clothes stripped to the bare bone: strapless tube dresses, backless T-shirts and slinky metallic gowns in nude, suntan, grey, brown, black and red. A sleek trouser suit and throw-on cover-all jacket completed the look. Kors added texture with punched suede patterning and a sliver of a snakeskin leather belt at the waist.

Show
Spring/Summer
1997

Date/Time
October 1996

Place
The Tent
Bryant Park
6th Avenue at 41st Street
New York

Format/Size
Paper
28cm x 21.5cm
(11in x 8½in)

Chanel

Karl Lagerfeld is not only one of the most prolific designers in the fashion industry – along with his role as creative director of Chanel, he also finds time to design collections for Fendi and his own eponymous line – but he is also a keen illustrator and photographer. Not surprising then that the invitations and press packs for each new collection serve to showcase several of his talents.

Each season Lagerfeld likes to select a muse who usually opens and closes the fashion show, and for this one the designer photographed the exquisite English model Karen Elson, whose startling copper red hair and alabaster complexion made her an unusual selection for the grand Parisian fashion house. However, Lagerfeld's collections are just as likely to be inspired by raw urban street style as they are by the rarefied world of Chanel's rue Cambon salon. This season, Lagerfeld illustrated his diverse collection of inspirations that included German Expressionism, military uniforms and the 1920s. Elson is also now a recording artist.

Show
Autumn/Winter
1997–98

Date/Time
12th March 1997
10.30am

Place
Carrousel du Louvre
99 rue de Rivoli
Paris

Format/Size
Card
18cm x 18cm
(7in x 7in)

Collette Dinnigan

Born in South Africa, based in Australia, Collette Dinnigan launched her label of luxury, dry-clean-only lingerie and lingerie-look dresses in 1990. In 1995 she was invited to show her designs in Paris by the Chambre Syndicale du Prêt-à-Porter des Couturiers et des Créateurs de Mode on the official catwalk show schedule. Her romantic, antique-looking designs proved an instant hit – Dinnigan was one of the key designers who promoted the trend for underwear-style outerwear. Over the years she has focused steadfastly on her trademark style and her delicate lace slip dresses, often lavishly embroidered, became a hit with Hollywood actresses such as Angelina Jolie, Naomi Watts and Halle Berry. She remains the biggest designer success story to come out of Australia. The image of the orange dress featured on the invitation by Canadian artist Shelagh Keeley is similar to a series of 14 paintings called "Fragrance de Tendresse", completed by Keeley between 1998 and 2000.

Show
Autumn/Winter
1997–98

Date/Time
10th March 1997
1.30pm

Place
Espace Carole de Bona
9 place des Petits Pères
Paris

Format/Size
Card
21cm x 15cm
(8¼in x 6in)

automne - hiver 97

English Eccentrics

BLUR ROSES Organza column dress

The English Eccentrics label was launched in 1983 by Helen David, her sister Judy Purbeck and their friend Claire Angel. Together, the trio created flamboyant silhouettes, showcasing unique textile prints that combined historical, architectural, art and fantasy imagery. This collection was inspired by *À Rebours* ("Against Nature"), the nineteenth-century novel by J-K. Huysmans, which, when published, was declared wickedly decadent.

For the invitation, the designers appropriated the quote, "tired of artificial flowers aping real ones, he wanted some natural flowers that would look like fakes", and this translated as prints featuring metallic lilies, computer-generated and Man Ray-inspired photographic blooms. The illustration by Camilla Dixon featured an organza dress printed with a design called "Blur Roses". English Eccentrics previously referenced Dada and Surrealism for a catwalk show in 1986, when the models wore lobster pot hats. There was no show this season, so the invitation promoted the exhibition located in the grounds of the Natural History Museum.

Show
Spring/Summer
1996

Date/Time
September 1995

Place
Main Show Tent
Natural History Museum
Cromwell Road
London

Format/Size
Paper
29.5cm x 21cm
(11½in x 8¼in)

Christian Lacroix. Luxe Hiver 90/91

Christian Lacroix. Collection Prêt-à-porter Printemps-Été 1992

Christian Lacroix

Show
Various

Date/Time
Various

Place
Paris

Format/Size
Card
21cm x 15cm
(8¼in x 6in)

Christian Lacroix appeared on the French fashion season in the early1980s when he was appointed designer-in-chief at the house of Patou. He has been heralded as single-handedly reviving the dying art of couture and after just a few much-lauded collections was bankrolled by businessman Bernard Arnault to launch his eponymous couture house. The timing was fortuitous as the buoyant economy saw demand for garments that reflected their hefty price tags. Clients not only wanted to feel like the million dollars they had spent, they wanted to look like it too.

Lacroix captured the prevailing mood for ostentation and flamboyance with showy ensembles that often included vibrantly coloured fur and feathers, elaborate embroidery, colourful large-scale prints, fancy buttons and endless ribbons and bows (sometimes on the same outfit). They made the perfect choice for partying Nouvelle Society matrons such as Nan Kempner and Sao Schlumberger. Lacroix's lively illustrations were as characterful as his catwalk creations and each season these were included within the designer's promotional material.

Ashish

Ashish Gupta is a designer with a sense of humour. When asked to describe his look, he merrily answers, "Sequins, glamour, sportswear and more sequins." Gupta likes fashion to be lighthearted and lift the spirits. "Children Are Special" was a message printed on a sweatshirt featured in this collection. The sweatshirt was worn with a glittery 1950s ballerina-length skirt over leggings. Its charming sentiment perfectly encapsulated the ethos of the designer and specifically this collection, which was a clashing collage of colourful prints and appliqués. Multicoloured knitted stripes and squares were stitched onto a lace sweater, a coat and what looked like a jogging suit, and then there were polka dots and even a pastel coloured skeleton. The designer showed several other prints, including snakes and ladders, crazy musical notes and a smoking cigarette. Even wearing a shocking pink sweater, Gupta could not outshine his dazzling models when he joined them for the finale.

Show
Autumn/Winter
2005–6

Date/Time
14th February 2005
11.45am

Place
British Fashion Council Square
Battersea Park
Queenstown Road
London

Format/Size
Paper
28.5cm x 21.5cm
(11¼in x 8½in)

Worlds End

PUNKATURE was Malcolm McLaren and Vivienne Westwood's paean to the Hobo. Show notes declared, "Inside out! Back to front... Anarchy in the Black Country" and Westwood told the press how Hobos in America expressed a sense of freedom with no responsibility. Exploring this theme, she used tin lids as buttons, trousers were held up with tiny braces and there were slashed dresses with plaited rags. The catwalk was full of familiar faces from the London scene (made up by Yvonne Gold), usually to be found hanging out at the duo's Nostalgia of Mud store. They wore sloppy patchwork knits, cut-up stretch satin and jersey tube skirts, and billowing dresses topped with giant, topless straw hats. Other dresses featured a film still print from *Blade Runner*, as did the programme.

For this show, McLaren draped the Pillar Hall's classical columns with graffitied banners. He shared credit alongside producer Mark Tabard. This collection was shown again, a week later, on a catwalk in Paris.

Show
Spring/Summer
1983

Date/Time
13th October 1982
5.30pm

Place
Pillar Hall
Olympia
Hammersmith Road
London

Format/Size
Paper
29.5cm x 21cm
(11¾in x 8¼in)

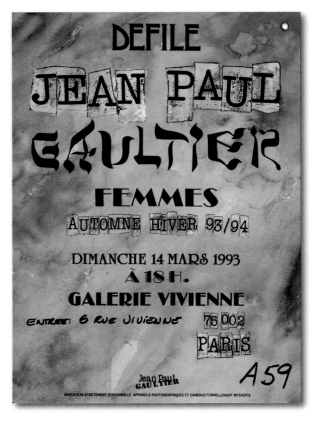

Jean Paul Gaultier

Even though Gaultier was showing womenswear, the invitation combined two portraits of men: an acetate of Sex Pistols' singer Johnny Rotten overlaid onto an unidentified Hasidic rabbi. These images, along with the ransom-note style script, identified two themes – punk and Jewish culture – that the designer combined in a collection that scandalized many parts of the fashion industry. Gaultier staged the show called "Chic Rabbis" in the nineteenth-century arcade next to his store in Rue Vivienne. Gold chairs outlined a red-carpet catwalk and the show was heralded by a live performance of traditional Jewish music and lit by giant Menorahs. The look drew heavily on the black tailored ensembles Gaultier had seen when he happened across a gathering of Hasidic Jews in New York. The satin coats, pin-stripe tailoring and fringe Argyle knits were accessorized with trademark ringlets and circular shtreimel fur hats. Gaultier added nose rings, Mohawk hairdos, giant trapper hats and kilts to the mix.

Show
Autumn/Winter
1993–94

Date/Time
14th March 1993
6pm

Place
Galerie Vivienne
6 rue Vivienne
Paris

Format/Size
Card, acetate
29.5cm x 21cm
(11¾in x 8¼in)

AUTOMNE-HIVER 1994/95 • Lundi 7 Mars 1994 à 18h30 • École des Beaux-Arts – 14, rue Bonaparte, Paris VI • P.R. Michèle Montagne (1) 42 03 91 00 • Showroom 6, rue de Braque Paris III (1) 48 87 37 47

Show
Autumn/Winter
1994–95

Date/Time
7th March 1994
6.30pm

Place
Ecole des Beaux-Arts
14 rue Bonaparte
Paris

Format/Size
Paper
28.5cm x 42cm
(11¼in x 16½in)

Martine Sitbon

Often described by the French press as a "British style designer", Martine Sitbon merrily embraced the edgy mood of London street style, melding it with her own version of something more handcrafted and historical. This approach is illustrated in the invitation, with its crayon scrawl, craft lesson stitching and sticky dots (often used on invitations to denote rank and placement), along with safety pins and the childish teddy, now looking a tad more threatening. Her designs were an equally eclectic mix of the old and the new, desirable and dark, often clashing head on. This collection continued her obsession with a raffish Dickensian silhouette cut in velvet and brocade, offset with more formal pin-stripe suiting and wool plaid. Fur and sheepskin added a luxurious feel, while mohair and Lurex sweaters were a nod to the King's Road c.1977. Sitbon ended the show with a series of bustle-style black lace dresses and colourful Chinese silk ensembles flamboyantly edged in fur and feathers.

John Galliano

"Too Rich Too Walk" was a Galliano show one could read as social commentary – the designer unravelling the clash of rich and poor, good and bad taste. The nod to grunge, the trailing hems and raw finish were reflected in the soundtrack as Nirvana crosscut with 1960s jukebox favourites by The Beach Boys, The Mamas and The Papas and The Shangri-las. The show ripped apart bourgeois classics (tweed suits and trench coats) and ended with a model in a psychedelic toilet-holder ball gown with teddy-bear balloon floating aloft, serenaded by Jackie Lee's children's TV show theme tune, "White Horses". Lilly Pulitzer-meets-Liz Taylor florals juxtaposed with Galliano's newspaper print were accessorized with festival-style fairy wings and old lady flowery hats, courtesy of milliner Stephen Jones. Later, he created hats made from swimming-pool inflatables referencing the Florida crazies who sit in their pastel-perfect homes, with plastic covering their chintz furniture in case neighbours stop by, heads covered in tinfoil, should aliens drop in. Beaded T-shirt dresses featured images from the invitation.

Show
Spring/Summer
2005

Date/Time
9th October 2004
8pm

Place
Théâtre de l'Empire
37 avenue de Wagram
Paris

Format/Size
Paper
20cm x 20cm
(7¾in x 7¾in)

Antonio Berardi

Show
Autumn/Winter
1999–2000

Date/Time
1st March 1999
9pm

Place
Via Vivaio, 7
Milan

Format/Size
Card
12cm (4¾in) diameter

Although Antonio Berardi was born and raised in the UK and made his name at London Fashion Week, in 1999 he decided to return to his Italian roots – his parents were Sicilians who moved to Britain in the 1950s. For his debut show during Milan Fashion Week, sandwiched on the schedule between Prada and Gucci, Berardi pulled out all the stops. The theme of this collection, called "Never Mind The Borgias", clashed the two cultures – the British punk spirit (the title was borrowed from the Sex Pistols) with the religious heritage of Italy. The catwalk, shaped like a giant crucifix, dripped with candle wax, while the air was heavy with incense. Angelic choirboys appeared alongside models with ornate Renaissance-style hairdos, wearing sequined bondage kilts, giant safety pins and a zip suit, all referencing punk. Another leather ensemble featured the words "FASHION SUCKS" in ransom-note cutout letters. The finale outfit, modelled by Mariacarla Boscono, was a barely-there fishnet gown made decent with curlicue embroidery.

Miu Miu

The mood for this collection was set by the glowing neon graphics of the invitation. Whether luminous ambient TV interference or flashing signage caught in acid rain, the radiant feel was replicated in the designer's use of shiny fabrics, from patent leather to quilted satin. At the start of the show model Karen Elson marched out in a nude coloured raincoat accessorized with an oversized sou'wester hat. She was quickly followed by Jacquetta Wheeler, wearing the same headgear, this time with thigh-length patent waders. The mood of the collection was resolutely outdoorsy, from Alison Goldfrapp's breathy sexed-up version of "Let's Get Physical" on the soundtrack to the salt'n'pepper knits, zippy ski salopettes and silk anoraks coloured forest green, tomato or mustard. Miuccia Prada loves a contradiction, so transposed anonymous utilitarian garments into desirable evening options and teamed a pussybow blouse and hotpants with her *accessory du jour*: a peaked ranger's cap.

Show
Autumn/Winter
2002–3

Date/Time
5th March 2002
5pm

Place
Via Fogazzaro, 36
Milan

Format/Size
Paper
25.5cm x 33.5cm
(10in x 13¼in)

Show
Autumn/Winter
1987–88

Date/Time
20th March 1987
6pm

Place
Halle de la Villette
Porte de Pantin
Paris

Format/Size
Card
16cm x 22cm
(6¼in x 8½in)

Jean Paul Gaultier

A notable thread running through the work of Jean Paul Gaultier is the designer's steadfast championing of difference on his catwalks. His shows have featured models of every age, shape, creed and colour. For this show Gaultier celebrated the ultimate alien, a glamorous green Martian. The collection, called "Forbidden Gaultier", refers to *Forbidden Planet,* a favourite childhood sci-fi film.

Models, including Mimi Potworowska and Eugenie Vincent, wore astronaut helmets, rubber swim caps and moulded wigs. Collaged outfits were a post-modern trip through Gaultier's universe: fetish dresses were chopped short, hemmed with a taffeta flounce or two and trimmed with a swathe of velvet and a handful of ostrich feathers. An hourglass jacket referencing Dior's New Look was constructed of rubber, Aran knit, leopard skin and tartan. Russian Space Race graphics decorated metallic second-skin tops and leggings.

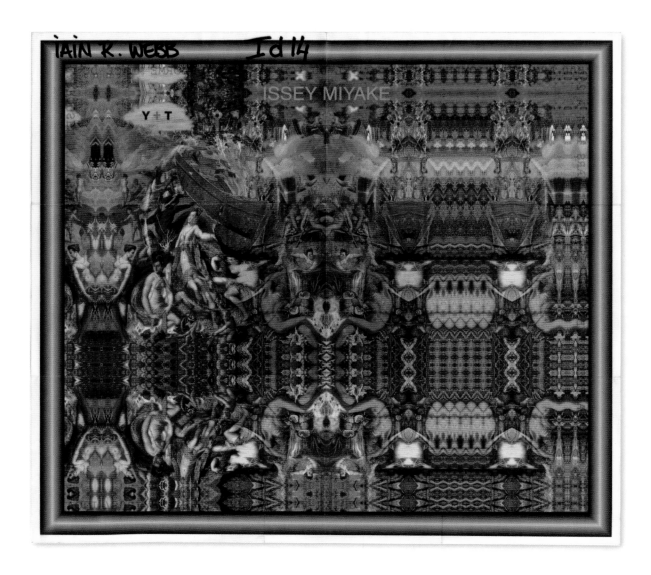

ISSEY MIYAKE

Issey Miyake

In the front row of Issey Miyake's show was the cast of Robert Altman's 1994 *Prêt-à-Porter* movie, including Lauren Bacall, Kim Basinger, Tracy Ullman, Rupert Everett and Sophia Loren, who wore the kind of large picture hat that you wouldn't want to sit behind. Like Loren's hat, filming threatened to overshadow the season but Miyake was having none of that as he presented a little performance of his own. Models wearing a mix of monochromatic, colourful, floral, metallic and pleated ensembles stepped off the catwalk into the audience. Then there were Miyake's hats. First, a mime duo ate their hats, which were made of cake. This was followed by hats made from pasta, bread and rice paper, pleated parasol-type hats, Tiffany lampshade hats, garbage bin hats, grass hats and even hats featuring lit candles that elicited a chorus of "Happy Birthday" from the photographers. Miyake's myriad ideas had the photographers clicking in his direction rather than towards the front row celebrities. No wonder he was smiling when he took his final bow.

Show
Autumn/Winter
1994–95

Date/Time
7th March 1994
8pm

Place
Carrousel du Louvre
99 rue de Rivoli
Paris

Format/Size
Paper
32cm x 35.5cm
(12½in x 14in)

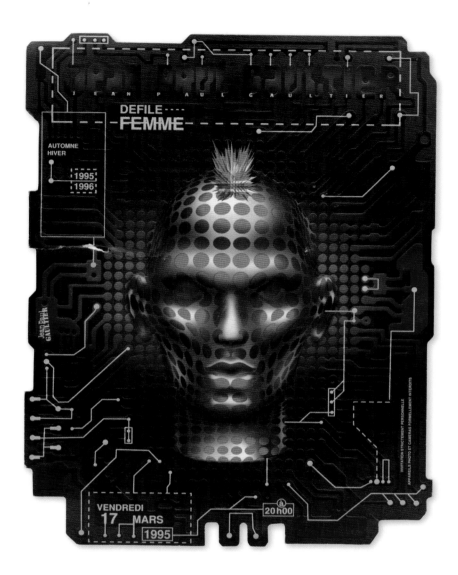

Show
Autumn/Winter
1995–96

Date/Time
17th March 1995
8pm

Place
Le Trianon
80 boulevard de
Rochechouart
Paris

Format/Size
Card
27cm x 20cm
(10½in x 8in)

Jean Paul Gaultier

Being a designer with one eye firmly fixed on the future, Jean Paul Gaultier has, throughout his career, been inspired time and again by robots and androids. He has also designed sci-fi costumes for Pedro Almodóvar's *Kika* (1993) and Luc Besson's *The Fifth Element* (1997). This collection took its cue from films such as *Mad Max*, *The Terminator* and *TRON*, a darker, discombobulated place, played out to a noisy, hard rock soundtrack provided by a DJ in a gantry above the catwalk. Gaultier invaded the graphic world of computer games with digital-dotted bodysuits and complex circuit-board knitwear mimicking the invitation. Models wore Cubist-style eye make-up that further emphasized the dystopian mood.

Gaultier kicked eveningwear into the future, offering oversized fur-trimmed velvet parkas and gowns with detachable trains. A series of inflatable nylon evening dresses in orange, pink and lime resembled a cross between sleeping bags and weather balloons. The final look featured a hat inflated by a hand-held hairdryer.

ANTONI ALISON

Antoni & Alison

To celebrate the thirteenth anniversary of their Antoni & Alison label, designers
Antoni Burakowski and Alison Roberts decided to explore the dark side in their
collection. For their invitation, the pair dressed themselves as disturbingly realistic
Goths. They also appeared in a film that was projected behind their models. The
design duo have continually shied away from the usual catwalk presentations
and garnered a cult following for their performance art-style productions staged
for several seasons in the lecture theatre at the V&A. These shows involved multimedia, including films, slideshow, installation, music and a voice-over of surreal
phrases and bon mots written by Roberts, which this particular season included,
"You don't waste your time on this". The collection featured T-shirts printed with
"STRANGE" and "STUPID".
    Other favoured venues included the Royal Court Theatre, the Shaftesbury
Theatre and the sculpture studio of the Chelsea Art School. A more recent show
(Autumn/Winter 2012) was called "Models Walking Up and Down in Dresses".

Show
Spring/Summer
2001

Date/Time
25th September 2000
5.15pm

Place
The Lecture Theatre
Victoria & Albert Museum
Exhibition Road
London

Format/Size
Card
15cm x 21cm
(6in x 8¼in)

Show
Spring/Summer
1986

Date/Time
17th October 1985
2.30pm

Place
Salle Medicis
Jardin de Tuileries
Paris

Format/Size
Tissue paper
72cm x 96cm
(28¼in x 37¾in)

Yohji Yamamoto

This large-scale invitation, tissue paper printed with dense black ink that seeped around the edges, arrived in a black shiny envelope. Only the designer's initial was scripted in white. Imagery such as this was still shockingly new, so as the audience took their seats and tried to peer over the photographers crowded several deep around the catwalk's edge, excitement levels were high. The Japanese designer's ragamuffin models with fake dreadlocks (the soundtrack was a mix of reggae, folk and classical) or tumbling manes under giant-sized berets and peaked caps looked equally startling in clothes that folded, wrapped and sometimes appeared trapped around the body, occasionally falling off. Editors noted oversized jackets, apron-like skirts, slashed sweaters, trailing hemlines and flapping shirttails, but among the black and white ensembles were flashes of colour – golden sand, silver, green and burnt orange. Despite the provocative spirit of this show there was an underlying romance in the clothes that has been evident in Yamamoto's collections down the decades.

Gareth Pugh

At this time the hype surrounding the young British designer had reached fever pitch and it seemed like the entire fashion world fought to get into Pugh's show, which started with a bang, literally, as a giant balloon that filled the entrance to the catwalk burst dramatically to screams of delight from the audience. The theatricality continued with the first model's head encased in a cube of Swarovski crystal; others wore extravagant rubber headdresses. Pugh is a showman who enjoys constructing extraordinary imagery that pushes the boundaries – one dress featured vast American football-style shoulder pads, another a collar of white mink rats. King of Pop Michael Jackson (someone who certainly understood the power of image) was referenced with glittering ankle socks and fingerless gloves worn throughout.

Pugh's all-black collection (highlighted by the shiny black invitation) included shredded leather, caveman fur and S&M hardware. It represented a new, exciting mood bubbling up in London that one fashion buyer described as "extreme individuality".

Show
Spring/Summer
2008

Date/Time
16th September 2007
3.45pm

Place
British Fashion Council Tent
Natural History Museum
Cromwell Road
London

Format/Size
Plastic
21cm x 21cm
(8¼in x 8¼in)

Alexander McQueen

Alexander McQueen's name has become synonymous with the concept fashion show. This show was called "La Poupée", inspired by the surreal dolls of 1930s artist Hans Bellmer (seen on the invite), and was staged in the Royal Horticultural Halls. Models descended a staircase worthy of 1930s film director Busby Berkeley to parade on a catwalk that was actually a trough of water several inches deep. Wearing Perspex platform shoes they appeared to walk on the surface.

McQueen's designs were as startling as the presentation: fondant-coloured brocades and stark white silks were spray-canned with fluorescent paint or slashed with zips. But the headline-making moment was when the designer sent out model Debra Shaw with her arms and legs shackled to a metal frame, not only making it difficult for her to walk but equally uncomfortable to watch. That Shaw was black caused a storm of protest from the more politically correct members of the press. McQueen instinctively knew how to push buttons.

Show
Spring/Summer
1997

Date/Time
27th September 1996

Place
Royal Horticultural Hall
80 Vincent Square
London

Format/Size
Card
21cm x 14.5cm
(8¼in x 5¾in)

Meadham Kirchhoff

Edward Meadham and Benjamin Kirchhoff are adept at crafting a complete world. A collaged invitation featuring bloodied hands arrived in an envelope printed with lovebirds, at odds with the image on this credit sheet. On the reverse was a veiled creature of indeterminate gender, surrounded by the words "WALL FLOWER", which also appeared in the presentation, scrawled on a model's forehead.

The pair's menswear installation presented a heartfelt narrative of decadence, punkish delight and despair. Androgynous boys lolled amid picnic chairs, pizza boxes, camp beds, twee table lamps and empty crisp packets, wearing a jumble of clothes topped with wrestler-style masks and knitted beanies; an electric blue chiffon dress was worn by a lad with matching hair and eyebrows. The casting by Matthew Josephs was genius! Meadham Kirchhoff offered a totally sensorial experience, including soundtrack (curated by ex-Blitz club kid Jeffrey Hinton), fragrance (the heady "Hammam Bouquet" from Penhaligon's) and flowers (trailing roses and orchids by Nikki Tibbles at Wild at Heart).

Show
Menswear
Spring/Summer
2013

Date/Time
17th June 2012
12pm

Place
Fashion East Space
Carlton House
3 Carlton Gardens
London

Format/Size
Paper
15cm x 21cm
(6in x 8¼in)

Suzy Menkes

Show
Autumn/Winter
1993–94

Date/Time
March 1993

Place
Paris

Format/Size
Badge
5.5cm (2in) diameter

During the Autumn/Winter 1993–94 shows, Suzy Menkes, then fashion editor of the *International Herald Tribune*, handed out this badge to her front row colleagues. It was the season after Marc Jacobs had presented his grunge-inspired collection for Perry Ellis in New York, a display that would get him fired.

Menkes was not a fan of the grunge aesthetic that included elongated T-shirt dresses, long diaphanous shirts, striped suits, crop tops, skinny "poor boy" knits, checkered shirts and floaty floral tea dresses, all worn with army boots and knitted beanies. Menkes, who had the badges made in Camden Market, remembers, "giving a badge to Anna [Wintour], who responded, Grunge is Garbage." Reviewing the grunge look in retrospect, Menkes believes it appeared shocking because it was the first time in her fashion lifetime that something so deliberately ugly was worn publicly. "But I do think that grunge led to Miuccia Prada's 'ugly aesthetic' and had much more influence on fashion than could have been imagined at the time," she said.

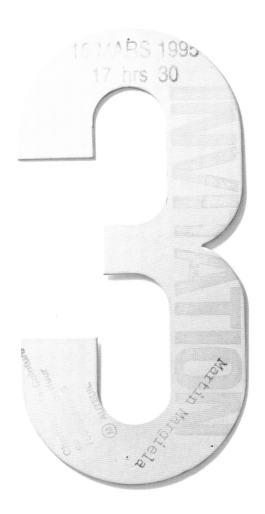
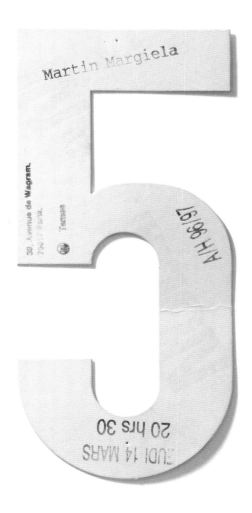

Maison Martin Margiela

Maison Martin Margiela employed these cut-out cardboard numbers for several seasons. They were used to denote where the guest would be seated. This no-frills, bare-bones approach has always been at the heart of the Margiela brand. Here, the information is rubber-stamped by hand. Margiela also uses this pragmatic approach for the labels stitched inside his clothes. It is not so surprising that the designer who has snubbed publicity throughout his career and shunned posing for promotional portraits should consistently shroud his models' identity. In his Autumn/Winter 1995 show he wrapped the models heads in fabric, while for Autumn/Winter 1996 the top half of each girl's face was painted black. This shaded effect was enhanced by the lighting as each model was followed by an attendant holding aloft a giant spotlight, which illuminated them alone. Most recently, models have worn jewel-encrusted masks completely encasing their heads. One such mask was later worn by rapper Kanye West.

Show
Autumn/Winter 1995–6
Autumn/Winter 1996–7

Date/Time
15th March 1995, 5.30pm
14 March 1996, 8.30pm

Place
Chemin de Ceinture, Paris
39 avenue de Wagram, Paris

Format/Size
Card
21.5cm x 10cm
(8½in x 4in)

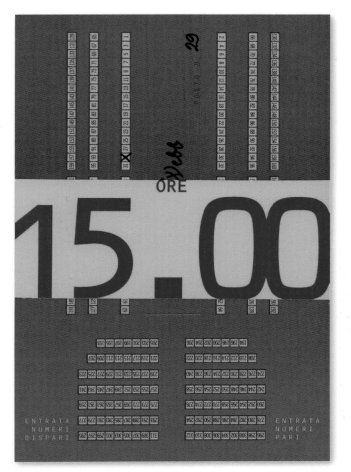

Show
Autumn/Winter
1999–2000

Date/Time
1st March 1999
3pm

Place
Via Borgonuovo, 11
Milan

Format/Size
Card
16cm x 11cm
(6¼in x 4¼in)

Emporio Armani

In Italy, Giorgio Armani is fashion. When fashion editors arrive at Linate Airport to attend the Milan leg of the international show season they are immediately welcomed with a giant Emporio Armani logo looming large over the arrivals hall. Jump in a taxi and ask for via Borgonuovo and the driver will reply: "Armani?" Before the designer decided to build himself a theatre in another part of the city the location for Armani's shows were in the basement of his home. Appropriate really, as there appears to be no differentiation between work and play in the Armani household and this ethic spills over onto the catwalk with the designer presenting an entire lifestyle brand. In a traditional format Armani sends out models (often in pairs, wearing a slight variation on a design) first in daywear, through cocktail to full-blown evening gowns, often heavily beaded.

For Autumn/Winter 1999–2000, the millennium was obviously on the designer's mind, with clothes featuring futuristic zips and tab fastenings. He also favoured block colours, turquoise and red, as featured on the invitation.

Kenzo

Kenzo Takada was among the first of the Japanese designers to present his vibrantly youthful fashion in the French capital in 1970, and he quickly acquired a cult following who battled with press and buyers to get into his shows. The designer brought a sense of fun and theatrics to the catwalks of Paris that best showcased his colourful, joyful creations. Within a decade he became one of the most influential and copied designers on Planet Fashion. In 1982 he opened a store in London. This invitation highlighted Kenzo's love of ethnic dress and traditional national costume – the patterned headscarf was a favourite accessory. The collection continued his clash of colourful peasant prints, tweeds and flannels alongside big, blousey florals, checks and stripes. This show, in an anonymous cavernous tent in the shadow of the Louvre, was no less eclectic, featuring the Kenzo family – male models appeared alongside female mannequins and even children (as indicated by this invitation). The show ended with the model Sayoko Yamaguchi appearing as a bride, her flower-strewn, poker-straight hair doubling as a train, stretching the entire length of the catwalk.

Show
Autumn/Winter
1982–83

Date/Time
31st March 1982
6pm

Place
Palais du Louvre
Paris

Format/Size
Card
15.5cm x 10.5cm
(6in x 4in)

Show
Spring/Summer
2013

Simone Rocha

Date/Time
18th September 2012
12pm

The rise of Simone Rocha, daughter of the British designer John Rocha, has been meteoric. In 2010 she showed her MA collection as part of the Central Saint Martins graduation show at London Fashion Week. Within a year she was presenting her own solo show to critical acclaim. Her look is relentlessly youthful and modern (innovative fabrics are her trademark), tinged with an air of nostalgia. The location pictured on the invitation is a local lane in Dublin, where the teenage Rocha went courting after school. It was also referenced in the grassy bank set on either side of her catwalk. This collection featured her signature prim tailoring, sweet broderie dresses and boyish suits in milky whites, buttercream, coffee, gold and black offset with rebellious hits of lemon, lime and pink. Her models wore Perspex-soled, lace-up shoes and crocheted halo headbands.

Place
Courtyard Show Space
Somerset House
The Strand
London

Later in the year Rocha won the Emerging Talent Award – Womenswear at the British Fashion Awards.

Format/Size
Card
14.5cm x 21cm
(5¾in x 8¼in)

Vivienne Westwood

The frolicking Satyr (half man, half goat) pictured on the invitation gave a hint of the Bacchanalian mood of this Gold Label collection called "Summertime". This was certainly Westwood at her most frisky. Models, dressed (or at times more *undressed*) in skew-whiff clothing and with "pulled-through-a-hedge-backwards" hairstyles, teetered on Westwood's vertiginous heels that alluded to the designer's desire to put women on a pedestal to be worshipped. This collection was a celebration of the sexual awakening of pubescent girls, referencing the mood of the movie, *Picnic at Hanging Rock* (1975). White cotton virginal-looking dresses were marked indelibly with tell-tale grass and red wine stains, the result perhaps of picnic pleasures. Toile de Jouy-type prints were twisted and draped on dresses with comely embonpoint necklines draped perilously low. Heaving bosoms were trapped in Westwood's trademark corsets, while her clever seaming clung to every curve. The look was accessorized with straw sun hats in a nod to the style featured in Gainsborough's painting, *Mr and Mrs Andrews* – another favourite of Westwood.

Show
Spring/Summer
2000

Date/Time
8th October 1999
2.30pm

Place
Jeu de Paume
1 place de la Concorde
Paris

Format/Size
Card
10cm x 21.5cm
(3¾in x 8½in)

Printemps / Eté 2013 Comme des Garçons Junya Watanabe Man
Le vendredi 29 juin 2012 à 10h Maison des Métallos Salle Claire 94 rue Jean-Pierre Timbaud 75011 Paris
Comme des Garçons S.A.S 10 place Vendôme 75001 Paris Tel 01 47 03 60 90 / 01 47 03 60 90

JUNYA WATANABE
COMME des GARÇONS
MAN

Show
Menswear
Spring/Summer
2013

Date/Time
29th June 2012
10am

Place
Maison des Métallos
94 rue Jean-Pierre
Timbaud
Paris

Format/Size
Poster
31cm x 47cm
(12¼in x 18½in)

Junya Watanabe

The moody landscape scene pictured on the invitation depicting hazy sunshine reflected across water also reflected the gentle nature of Watanabe's presentation in this airy gallery space. The audience sat at little tables as though chilling at a street café, as models casually sauntered by, wearing skinny summery suits with half-mast trousers revealing bare ankles tucked into creamy Converse sneakers. Throughout the show several models took their jackets off to show their shirts patterned with sweet Liberty-style prints or fresh-looking stripes. There were identifiably British references throughout the collection from artist David Hockney in his baker boy flat cap through to foppish Oxford college pupils punting lazily downstream in their red, white and blue ticking blazers outlined in contrast ribbon. The atmosphere (and the clothes themselves) was all very relaxed, with the acoustic Beatles soundtrack that featured "Blackbird", "The Two Of Us", "Mother Nature's Son" and "Here Comes The Sun" providing a charming end to a charming show.

Christopher Kane

Since his MA show at London's Central Saint Martins in 2006, Scotsman Christopher Kane had become the go-to London designer for bright, eye-popping colour. This collection, a volte-face to his Spring/Summer collection that featured circular cuts in orange, yellow, lime and peach, was a harder, more aggressive statement, "something bolder, stronger and not so pretty," the designer told journalists. So, this season Kane offered stripes of black velvet that corseted the body, alongside grey tweed cut into pencil skirts and matching zip cardigan jackets. The beetles pictured on the giveaway bag, designed by Kane, echoed the gleaming metallic sheen of his dresses that were a criss-cross of green, bronze and gold ribbons. And instead of teaming these sophisticated dresses with a pair of glamorous high heels, Kane put his models in flat, black lace-up brogues worn with an ankle sock, and added a grey cashmere sweater or a Prince of Wales check sweatshirt for an edgier look.

Show
Autumn/Winter
2009–10

Date/Time
22nd February 2009
12.45pm

Place
Topshop P3
University of Westminster
35 Marylebone Road
London

Format/Size
Tote bag
40.5cm x 36cm
(16in x 14¼in)

Show
Menswear
Spring/Summer
1988

Date/Time
9th–12th October
1987

Place
British Designer Show
Olympia
Hammersmith Road
London

Format/Size
Magazine
26cm x 18.5cm
(10¼in x 7¼in)

Dirk Bikkembergs

Dirk Bikkembergs made a big impression as one of the Antwerp Six, a group of graduates from the Antwerp Royal Academy of Fine Arts that caused a stir when they showed in London in 1986. His look is super sexy and tailored to the athletic, modern man, but while his aesthetic takes inspiration from "strong, healthy and virile" macho male stereotypes, he can't resist poking a little fun, too. His sense of humour and attention to detail is integrated throughout his work, from the collection here, entitled "My Daddy Is A Farmer", to the presentation and accompanying promotional material. In this instance the notification of his show dates is packaged in the kind of 10-cent trash title published by Popular Library. "The Chicken Farm" features cover lines such as "He couldn't be tamed…" and "The best dressed chicken farmer in the West". The cover features model Alain Gossuin holding a big cockerel, photographed by Karel Fonteyne. For later collections Bikkembergs has employed footballers and athletes to model his designs.

Vivienne Westwood

Following the catwalk shows, the press are invited to take a closer look at new collections on the rack in showrooms. Catwalk shows invariably feature an edited selection. Vivienne Westwood's Gold Label mainline collection, called "Get A Life" and also "Planet Gaia", was presented at her London flagship store. Originally shown in Paris, it was a tour de force for Westwood, who continued to use her cultural status to champion the anti-consumer, eco message that is dear to her heart. Models wore painted, raw-edged outfits decorated with slogans. The press release advocated eco warriors to "Dress Up!" and "Do-It-Yourself": "Go to art galleries … sign up to Prince Charles' Rainforest project".

   The designer took her bows wearing a T-shirt featuring the invitation's print, with a toy frog tucked under her shirt. A look from this collection was chosen by milliner Stephen Jones as 2010 Dress of the Year, at the Fashion Museum, Bath.

Show
Spring/Summer
2010

Date/Time
4th November 2009
10am–5pm

Place
44 Conduit Street
London

Format/Size
Card
17cm x 12cm
(6½in x 5¾in)

'ANGELS WITH DIRTY FACES'

THE STEPHEN LINARD COLLECTION

Mobsters
and
Dames

Convicts
and
Conmen

Cowboys
and
Tomboys

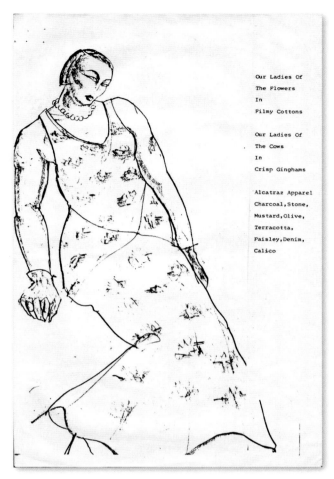

Our Ladies Of
The Flowers
In
Filmy Cottons

Our Ladies Of
The Cows
In
Crisp Ginghams

Alcatraz Apparel
Charcoal,Stone,
Mustard,Olive,
Terracotta,
Paisley,Denim,
Calico

Stephen Linard

Show
Spring/Summer 1983

Date/Time
October 1982

Place
Perry Ogden's Studio
50A Rosebery Avenue
London

Format/Size
Paper
33cm x 22.5cm
(13in x 8¾in)

Titled "Angels With Dirty Faces", this show was one of the defining moments in 1980s British fashion. In the airy third-floor photographic studio loaned by photographer Perry Ogden models slunk along in heavy shoes and flighty dresses inspired by Sissy Spacek in *Badlands* (1973). In the programme notes Linard listed other inspirations: Mobsters and Dames, Convicts and Conmen, Cowboys and Tomboys, Our Ladies Of The Flowers in Filmy Cottons, and Alcatraz Apparel.

Linard was one of the key faces on the New Romantic scene. A stalwart habitué of the Blitz nightclub, unsurprisingly there was a whiff of decadence among the stripes, paisleys and pretty tea-dance florals. The designer corralled his nightclubbing friends into collaborating – the programme exquisitely illustrated by Lee Sheldrick, a classmate at Saint Martin's School of Art, the soundtrack supplied by Jeffrey Hinton and the faces painted by Lesley Chilkes (who had done the same for many of Linard's squatting roommates). Even a few nightclub heartthrobs modelled, including Dylan Jones (now editor of *GQ*) and actor Daryl Humphries.

Yohji Yamamoto

This particular season Yohji Yamamoto's show appeared to be split in two: one half of the collection aimed at a 1960s schoolboy who yearned to be a Beatle, while the other half clothed his more outdoorsy American cousin. That meant striped Mod blazers, collarless jackets, narrow ties and mop-top hairdos (by Marc Lopez) versus fur collars, folksy patterned knits, hunting jackets and park ranger hats. Yamamoto has said that he finds designing menswear difficult because he doesn't like trendy, fashionable men and for this reason he has distanced himself from trends. Instead he has developed a customer base that is, for the most part, working in the creative arts and can enjoy wearing clothes imbued with his sense of fun. From childhood his dream was to be a painter and this is reflected in the sweeping, confident lines of his sketches that feature in this show programme.

   The year 1989 also saw the release of *Notebook on Cities and Clothes*, a film by director Wim Wenders, documenting Yamamoto's design process.

Show
Menswear
Autumn/Winter
1989–90

Date/Time
5th February 1989
2.30pm

Place
155 rue Saint-Martin
Paris

Format/Size
Paper
30cm x 21cm
(11¾in x 8¼in)

Show
Autumn/Winter
1987–88

Date/Time
22nd March 1987
12pm

Place
Salle Perrault
Cour Carrée du Louvre
Paris

Format/Size
Paper
42.5cm x 31cm
(16¾in x 12¼in)

Martine Sitbon

Martine Sitbon is a Parisian designer with a distinctly British – and more specifically, London – sensibility. Throughout her career she has lived and worked on the fringes of French fashion and this is often reflected on her catwalk. Her designs rework classic tailoring with a twist, quite literally, as illustrated on the invitation. This collection continued Sitbon's love affair with the Edwardian silhouette but for this particular showing the designer cleverly draped giant blooms among the folds of fabric, while little velvet dresses became walking bouquets. Ladylike touches included Eliza Doolittle picture hats and Grace Kelly-style handbags.

Along with her art director partner Marc Ascoli, whose collaborations with Japanese designer Yohji Yamamoto were tremendously influential in the 1980s, the pair became the pin-up power couple for the post-modernist generation. Sat alongside the fashion groupies, who were out in force at this show, were Jean Paul Gaultier, Rei Kawakubo of Comme des Garçons and Yamamoto himself.

Stephen Jones

Stephen Jones emerged at the beginning of the 1980s, championing a thoroughly old-fashioned idea of hat wearing for a thoroughly modern audience. Jones presented himself as a stylized idea of a milliner opening his own salon. By the end of the decade he had moved to a showroom in London's Soho, where he invited journalists and clients alike to view his new collections. Each season he unveiled these at the designer trade shows in London, Paris, Tokyo and New York. For his Autumn/Winter 1987–88 collection, boldly titled, "Stephen Jones World", the designer offered "a fantasy fashion voyage", with hats called "Minnie Ha Ha" and "Molly Brown". He also included some hats for men in this collection, from traditional tweed pork pie hats with upturned brims to nylon Leatherman peaked caps, trimmed with celluloid movie film. For his Autumn/Winter 2003–04 collection (opposite), titled "Poseur", the designer created hats inspired by his old New Romantic friends, "Gerlinde", "Kim", "Myra" and "Fiona" among others.

Show
Autumn/Winter
1987–88

Date/Time
March 1987

Place
34 Lexington Street
London

Format/Size
Paper
29.5cm x 21cm
(11½in x 8¼in)

Show
Autumn/Winter
2003–04

Date/Time
February 2003

Place
36 Great Queen Street
London

Format/Size
Paper
29.5cm x 21cm
(11½in x 8¼in)

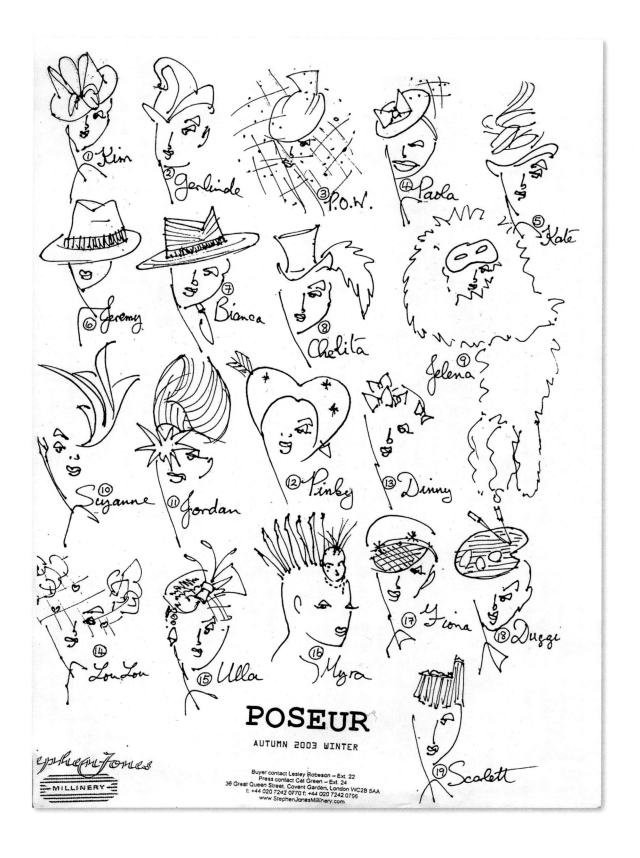

Wendy Dagworthy

Dagworthy, who established her label in 1972, used these posters to promote her static presentations at the Inn on the Park Hotel in London. At this time she was also creating stage costumes for cult glam group Roxy Music. In the 1980s Dagworthy was part of a group of designers, including Katharine Hamnett, Jasper Conran, Bodymap and Betty Jackson (Dagworthy's one-time assistant who illustrated the poster above right), that reinvigorated the British fashion scene. Her catwalk shows were joyful displays, featuring a cast of young models wearing her designs, which layered pattern and print and played with proportion. Throughout her career, Dagworthy has been heavily involved in education and has been described as a "star spotter". In her roles as head of fashion at Central Saint Martins and Professor of Fashion at the RCA in London, she has mentored Stella McCartney, Erdem, Hussein Chalayan and Katie Eary among others. In January 2014 she announced her retirement.

Show
Autumn/Winter 1976–77
Autumn/Winter 1977–78

Date
8th–11th April 1976
31st March–3rd April 1977

Place
Inn on the Park
Park Lane
London

Format/Size
Posters
55.5cm x 37.5cm
(22in x 14¾in)
50cm x 37.5cm
(19¾in x 14¾in)

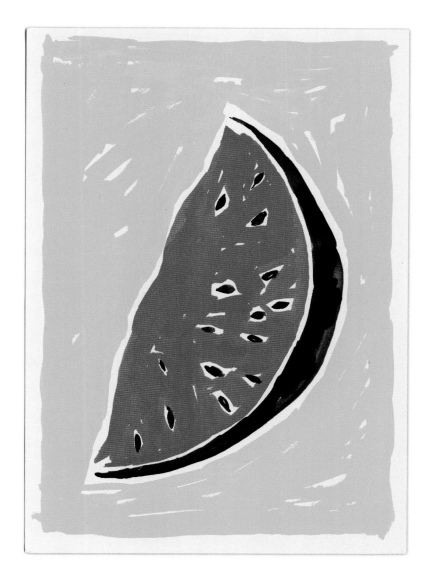

Show
Menswear
Spring/Summer 1990

Date/Time
31st August 1989
5.30pm

Place
Opéra Comique
Salle Favart
1 place Boïeldieu
Paris

Format/Size
Card
21cm x 13cm
(8¼in x 6¾in)

Richard James

To celebrate the new decade a looser, relaxed mood moved into the menswear arena that ousted the Wall Street business suits with their wide-boy shoulders. This season British tailor Richard James emerged as a trailblazer as bright as the clothes he showed on his catwalk. James's colour palette took its cue from his invitation, a fruity menu of watermelon, lemon, lime, mandarin and grape. There were flowers too, including clematis embroidered shirts and giant sunflower prints planted on shorts, shirts and even an updated Nehru jacket. James was not a designer for shrinking violets! But the most radical (and popular) look offered by James and other leading menswear designers in Paris that season was the new suit that comprised an oversized jacket and equally roomy wide-stripe shorts. Due to their size these shorts inspired much debate as to whether they were in fact short trousers rather than long shorts, yet James was committed to the look, even showing an eveningwear version.

Meadham Kirchhoff

Edward Meadham and Benjamin Kirchhoff continue the legacy of designers such as Jean Paul Gaultier, Andre Walker and the late Franco Moschino, who have long since flouted convention and celebrated difference with a flourish and sense of fun. The utter joyfulness of the illustration on the invitation's envelope – the rainbow, fried eggs, fruit, flowers and unicorn – could easily have been lifted from stickers on a pre-pubescent's sacred diary and this exuberant mood translated directly to their catwalk, which even featured a light-up dance floor. All these motifs appeared as prints, appliqués or embroideries.

The ecstatic posturing and gaudy paintbox Picasso make-up in this collection (called "he gave me blue roses, LIFE, vicariously") took its cue from 1980s club icons such as Leigh Bowery, Trojan, Rachel Auburn and Mark Vaultier. Here, the designers merrily clashed tweed, tartans, Lurex and lace, checks, stripes and polka dots, while multicoloured sequin suits and furs would translate into coveted pieces for the duo's commercial collaboration with Topshop in the following year.

Show
Autumn/Winter
2012–13

Date/Time
21st February 2012
2pm

Place
Topshop
Old Billingsgate Market
Lower Thames Street
London

Format/Size
Envelope
11cm x 16cm
(4½in x 6¼in)

Show
Autumn/Winter
2008–9

Date/Time
14th February 2008
7.30pm

Place
The Old Sorting Office
21–31 New Oxford Street
London

Format/Size
Card
18cm x 12cm
(7in x 4¾in)

Vivienne Westwood

The return of Vivienne Westwood Red Label to the London Fashion Week schedule prompted banner headlines. Appropriate then that her show, staged in an abandoned post office in New Oxford Street, should begin with a model of indeterminate gender brandishing a protest-style placard questioning the fair trial of prisoners in Guantanamo Bay. Westwood, who is no stranger to shock and outrage, used the press coverage to highlight her latest political standpoint. Her line-up of models was a mix of punks, poseurs and posh girls – including Alice Dellal, Daisy Lowe, Coco Rocha and Jaime Winston (modelling Westwood's trademark horns). Although the clothes did have a crazy "Alice In Wonderland" look – the pin-stripe tailoring of the Mad Hatter (along with several mad hats!) and the crown of the Red Queen – there was no obvious link with the fancy costumed rabbits illustrated on the show and after-show party invitations.

Givenchy

In 1957 RCA student Sally Tuffin (later one half of fashion label Foale & Tuffin), won the Bianca Mosca Award from the Royal Society of Arts. In 1960 she used this bursary to travel with a friend around Spain, Italy and France, where she attended the haute couture shows in Paris. These included Nina Ricci, Pierre Cardin, Lanvin and Givenchy. Tuffin noted in her journal that Balenciaga "refuses any students now especially those from the Royal College of Art." Alongside her illustrations of the new collections Tuffin added her own critique. Ricci was deemed "a very bold adventurous show," Cardin offered a "very beautiful collection…reminiscent of the 30s" while at Lanvin evening dresses offered "a vague 20s look". Givenchy's sculptural coats and jackets were "concave front, convex back". Tuffin deemed his leather coats "the best in Paris", while dresses and suits in chenille were "very new and chic". Cocktail dresses featured beaded belts "more like fabulous necklaces" and evening dresses were "fantasies of imagination".

Show
Autumn/Winter 1960–61

Date/Time
April 1960

Place
3 avenue George V
Paris

Format/Size
Paper
29.7cm x 21cm
(11¾in x 8¼in)

GIVENCHY

Paris March 3Ith, 1960

SOCIÉTÉ ANONYME AU CAPITAL DE 2.500.000 FRANCS
3, AVENUE GEORGE V - PARIS (8e)
R.C.Seine 55 B 5122 — BAL. 92-60 À 92-62
COMPTE CHEQUE POST. PARIS 17 286 72

Miss Sally TUFFIN
II6, Queens Gate
LONDON

Dear Miss Tuffin,

    In answer to your letter of March 28th, we are sending you, herewith, an invitation card for you and your friend.

    Awainting the pleasure of seing you, we are,

        Very truly yours,

        Pour Jean Claude de GIVENCHY
        The secretary,

Worlds End

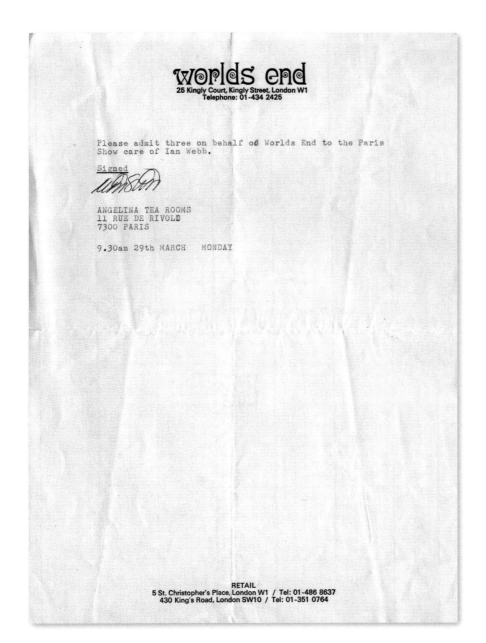

When Vivienne Westwood and Malcolm McLaren took their Buffalo girls and boys across the Channel to Paris their faithful followers hitched a ride. This was the first time the French had seen the pair's sartorial escapades first hand and it came as quite a shock. The normally polite and gentile atmosphere of the famous Parisian tearooms was shattered by the British invasion. A makeshift catwalk only a few feet wide was constructed down the middle of the venue, with the dancing models barely able to pass one another. Not surprising as the clothes were heavily layered – patchworked sheepskin jackets over hooded jersey shirts, padded skirts and toga dresses with trailing hems. In the programme Westwood suggested: "Take your mother's old brassière and wear it undisguised over your school jumper and have a muddy face". In the audience Japanese designer Issey Miyake, one of Westwood's staunchest supporters, smiled and clapped along as the catwalk collapsed during the finale.

Show
Autumn/Winter
1982–83

Date/Time
29th March 1982
9.30am

Place
Angelina Tea Rooms
11 rue de Rivoli
Paris

Format/Size
Paper
29.5cm x 21cm
(11½in x 8¼in)

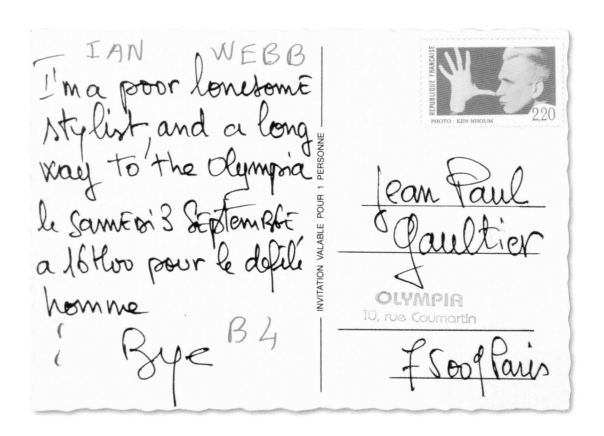

Jean Paul Gaultier

One of the most memorable moments in this show featured a posse of cowboys wearing black rubber cycling shorts, long evening gloves, backpacks and bandit-style bandanas. Other models, including Zane O'Donnell, Rick Giles and Cameron Alborzian, wore leopard-skin shorts, glittering chaps, brocade waistcoats, striped suits and pastel-coloured blazers, accessorized with scarves edged with silver coins. Children's-style cowboy hats were worn throughout.

This was a busy time for the designer, as the same year he also created the costumes for Peter Greenaway's film *The Cook, The Thief, His Wife & Her Lover*, and famously dressed Madonna for her "Blonde Ambition" World Tour that included his iconic conical corset. Pieces from this collection can also be viewed in the pop video directed by Jean-Baptiste Mondino accompanying Gaultier's rap record, "How To Do That". The stamp on the invitation showing Gaultier thumbing his nose parodied how he was so often depicted in the media as the enfant terrible of Paris Fashion.

Show
Menswear
Spring/Summer
1989

Date/Time
3rd September 1988
4pm

Place
Olympia
10 rue de Caumartin
Paris

Format/Size
Postcard
11cm x 15cm
(4¼in x 6in)

LOUIS VUITTON MALLETIER
101 CHAMPS ELYSEES PARIS

LOUIS VUITTON

PRIE

Monsieur Hywel Davies
ShowStudio

PLACE G III 8

PLIER ICI

D'ASSISTER A LA PRESENTATION
DE LA COLLECTION PRINTEMPS-ETE 2012

JEUDI 23 JUIN 2011 A 14H30

SERRE DU PARC ANDRE CITROEN
RUE DE LA MONTAGNE DE LA FAGE
PARIS 15e

SERVICE DE PRESSE TEL. 01 55 80 33 20

Show
Menswear
Spring/Summer 2012

Date/Time
23rd June 2011
2.30pm

Place
Serre du Parc André
Citroën
Paris

Format/Size
Airmail letter
19cm x 23.5cm
(7½in x 9in)

Louis Vuitton

The appointment of British designer Kim Jones as creative director at Louis Vuitton menswear in 2011 was cause for excitement. Jones, who had made his name fronting his edgy eponymous label in London, had already made the leap from cult brand to establishment when he was previously appointed designer-in-chief at Alfred Dunhill.

The designer's upbringing in Africa has instilled in him the travel bug that he delights in weaving into his collections and that suits the Vuitton client, whose jet-set, globetrotting lifestyle is central to the brand. The airmail letter invitation was another hint that Jones had travel on his mind. This collection was a curious mix of elegant and ethnic, traditional and quirky, so neatly tailored shawl-collared tuxedo suits were worn with the kind of rough leather sandals that might have been picked up on safari, while distinctive bright red and blue checked Masai scarves were cut into sporty sweaters and shorts.

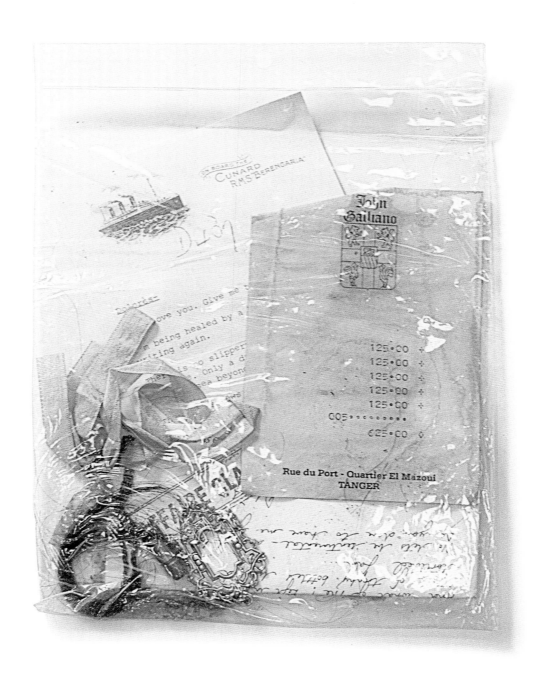

Show
Accessories
Spring/Summer
1988

Date/Time
16th–20th October 1987

Place
111–113 rue Saint Maur
Paris

Format/Size
Envelope containing
postcards
19cm x 12.5cm
(7½in x 5in)

Bernstock Speirs

Paul Bernstock and Thelma Speirs encapsulated a new-style designer who not only enjoyed the process of creating product (their fabulous, fun accessories), but were also determined to construct the total package around their designs – quite literally, in this case. The duo personally undertook the laborious task of putting together this press pack, from styling the shoot to meticulously water-staining the brown envelopes and sticking on stamps, franked by hand with a swish of gold pen. It was all part of the designer vision that was becoming crucially important in the business of fashion. This presentation of the total concept welcomed a new generation of would-be art directors and imagemakers. The collection took the travel theme throughout, with items given names of fashionable cities: a lace appliquéd scarf was called "Venice", a floral print bowler hat with a paper brim was "Rio", a satchel covered in travel stickers was "Tokyo" and a belt made from luggage labels, "New York". The photographs were by Mark Lewis.

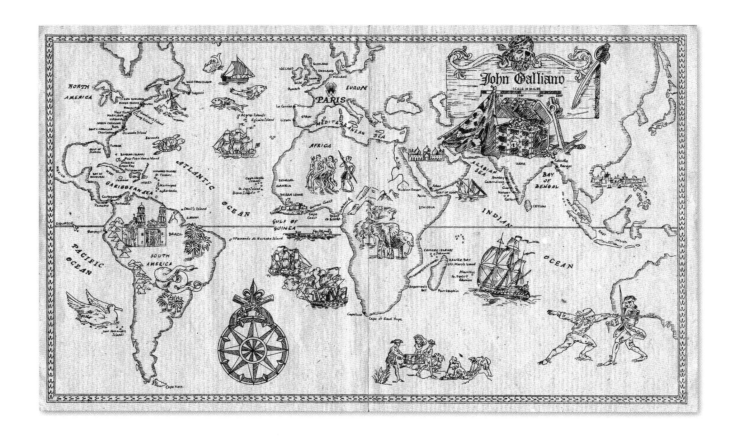

John Galliano

The designer's debut show in Paris was announced with a pirate's map. This madcap historical romp started with a deconstructed admiral's dress uniform featuring vast exaggerated epaulettes, worn over a skimpy flesh-coloured petticoat dress. The models elaborate raggle-taggle hairstyle looked not unlike like the remains of a sunken sailing ship. And so it went on, a maelstrom of twirling hems, bias cutting, Regency stripes, lace, tartan, faded florals, garters, ruffs and Wicked Lady Gainsborough hats complete with ostentatious ostrich feathers. Models, including Helena Christensen, Susie Bick and Yameen Ghauri, acted out Galliano's characterizations with much fluttering of eyelids, heaving bosoms and swooning to a soundtrack that mixed sea shanties with *Bladerunner* by Vangelis and dialogue from *Funny Face* ("You'll have to drug her to get her to Paris"). An ingénue Kate Moss in a shrunken jacket fashioned from a Union Jack made a perfect front-page picture.

Show
Spring/Summer
1993

Date/Time
14th October 1992
9pm

Place
Salle Wagram
39 avenue Wagram
Paris

Format/Size
Paper
19cm x 32cm
(7½in x 12½in)

Show
Autumn/Winter
1994–95

Date/Time
6th March 1994
8.30pm

Place
38 avenue Reille
Paris

Format/Size
Card
10cm x 16.5cm
(4in x 6½in)

Jean Paul Gaultier

For a designer with such an abundant back catalogue it is difficult to rate one show over another but even in a world used to hyperbole this has to be one of Jean Paul Gaultier's most extraordinary presentations. From the vast venue decorated with fake snow and twinkling lights to the idiosyncratic model casting, the show was a *tour-de-force* triumph. The train ticket invited guests to take a trip on the "Transoccidental Orient Express" and the designer didn't disappoint, offering a mix of richly patterned ensembles inspired by the national costumes worn by the indigenous people of Mongolia, Siberia, Tibet and Iceland. Musician Björk walked in the show, alongside a host of the designer's favourite models, including Eugenie Vincent, Rossy de Palma and Vladimir McCray, as well as friends from the industry, who received warm applause from their front-row colleagues. The collection was a sumptuous collage of blanket-wrap coats, fur pants, padded satin, velvet, sheepskin and voluminous hoods.

Home !!!

DKNY

The "Road Trip" theme cast the DKNY models as the coolest characters, even when temperatures soared in a summer heatwave. Against a panoramic backdrop that pictured an endless deserted highway they ventured on their journey with the car radio cranked up: a soundtrack that included The Rolling Stones' "Sympathy For The Devil", Tom Petty's "American Girl", Talking Heads' "Psycho Killer" and Iggy Pop's "The Passenger". Aviator sunglasses, army boots and a Downtown attitude combined for a mood that was part Desert Storm, part Sarah Connor – a little undone, like a button-through shirt-waister, leather blouson or straggly, surf hairdo. A handful of sequins gleamed like sun-kissed flesh. Wearing zesty lemon, orange, magenta and turquoise chiffon dresses thrown over cutaway swimsuits Karan's heroine took to the dancefloor of some low-rent discotheque on the outskirts of Nowheresville. This show offered the kind of clothes that could have walked off the runway and into the real world without missing a beat.

Show
Spring/Summer
2004

Date/Time
15th September 2003
5pm

Place
Eyebeam
540 West 21st Street
New York

Format/Size
Envelope containing postcards
10.5cm x 15cm
(4¼in x 6in)

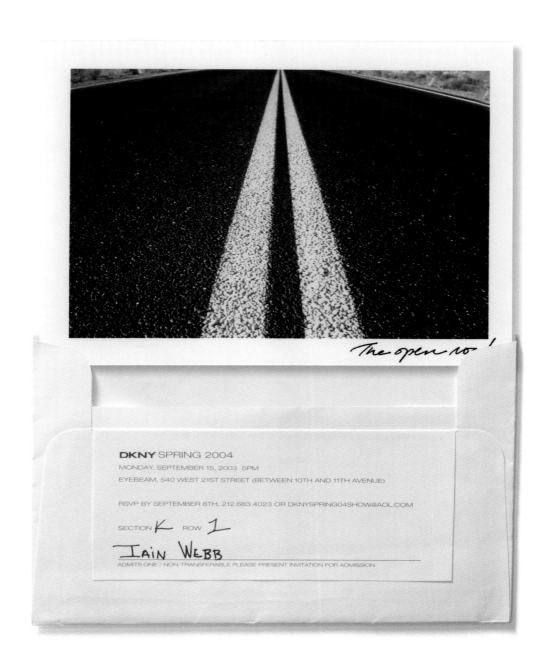

The open road!

DKNY SPRING 2004

MONDAY, SEPTEMBER 15, 2003 5PM

EYEBEAM, 540 WEST 21ST STREET (BETWEEN 10TH AND 11TH AVENUE)

RSVP BY SEPTEMBER 8TH, 212.683.4023 OR DKNYSPRING04SHOW@AOL.COM

SECTION K ROW 1

Iain Webb

ADMITS ONE / NON-TRANSFERABLE PLEASE PRESENT INVITATION FOR ADMISSION

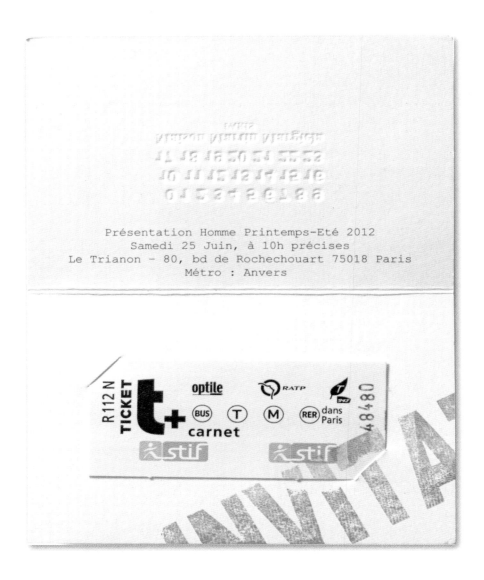

Présentation Homme Printemps-Eté 2012
Samedi 25 Juin, à 10h précises
Le Trianon - 80, bd de Rochechouart 75018 Paris
Métro : Anvers

Maison Martin Margiela

The genius of a designer like Martin Margiela is that he can make the straightforward feel strange. Although the designer himself had left the label in 2010, this was the template he had forged. This presentation was staged at Le Trianon theatre with models framed against a red velvet backdrop. At first glance the collection appeared equally as unchallenging, however on closer inspection a tailored jacket featured a subtle No. 10 football-style logo on the back and a tuxedo trouser substituted a satin stripe on the outside leg for a zip fastener. Tiny detailing is often what differentiates MMM designs, such as a slim pen pocket on the breast of a jacket or a clear plastic pocket for a phone (or travel card) on a trouser leg. An updated safari jacket continued the travel theme, as did a deconstructed red nylon anorak-cum-cape, still with the instantly recognizable go-faster stripes.

Show
Menswear
Spring/Summer
2012

Date/Time
25th June 2011
10am

Place
Le Trianon
80 boulevard de Rochechouart
Paris

Format/Size
Carnet ticket
13cm x 9.5cm
(5in x 3¾in)

Show
Spring/Summer
2000

Date/Time
23rd September 1999
8pm

Place
Sadler's Wells Theatre
Rosebery Avenue
London

Format/Size
Card
15cm x 15cm
(5¾in x 5¾in)

Hussein Chalayan

Although the photograph by David Hughes on the invitation features nine-year-old Lewis Dicker, son of Chalayan's pattern director, operating the kind of remote control device used to manoeuvre a toy airplane, nothing could have prepared the audience for the fabulous fashion moment ahead. During the show Dicker, wearing the same outfit and carrying the device, ambled coyly onto the set before crouching mysteriously to one side of the stage. He was joined by model Erika Wall, who posed centre-front. Wall's dress appeared to be fashioned from palest pink, shiny fibreglass and as Dicker flicked a switch on his control pad, a section of the dress opened like a jet plane's stabilizer fin. Another flick and back panels lifted to reveal a bustle-style petticoat of frothy tulle. Such collisions of design and science have become the cornerstone of Chalayan's design statement, from his early dresses patterned by his chemistry experiments to fully automated ensembles that morphed from one historical silhouette to another.

21 Shop

The opening of the 21 Shop at Woollands department store, a revolutionary retail concept offering young people clothes by young designers, was a momentous event in Swinging Sixties London. This was a collaboration with British *Vogue* magazine, the focus of the evening being the Young Idea fashion show featuring designers who included Foale and Tuffin and Gerald McCann, who would be stocked in the new 21 Shop. The show was promoted in *Vogue* with a 14-page fashion editorial. To celebrate the occasion the invitation promised champagne and The Temperance Seven, nine young jazz musicians borne out of the Royal College of Art, who would play while models including Jean Shrimpton and Celia Hammond danced through the store. The invitation was equally forward-thinking, a graphic tour de force featuring stylish portraits of Shrimpton photographed by David Bailey, along with bold red graphics that spelt out the excitement surrounding the event: Beyond! Swinging! Wild! and GAS! The interior of the 21 Shop was the work of upcoming designer Terence Conran.

Show
Store opening

Date/Time
14th September 1961
6.30pm and 9.30pm

Place
Woollands
Knightsbridge
London

Format/Size
Card
32.5cm x 47cm
(12¾in x 18½in)

GAS!

WOOLLANDS

21

Wolsey/Bailey

Woollands of Knightsbridge, Belgravia 6000

Woollands of Knightsbridge invite you to the Young Idea fashion show with Vogue to celebrate the opening of their new 21 Shop on Thursday September 14 at 6.30 and 9.30 pm / The Temperance Seven / Champagne Please write or ring for your ticket

Jean Paul Gaultier

The launch of the Galerie Gaultier store was a hot ticket because by this time the designer was viewed as the patron saint of London's fashion pack. The invitation featured a distressed metal plate. This striking verdigris effect, achieved by treating copper metal with acetic acid, was a style Gaultier used for his interiors that reflected the way he deconstructed fashion. Other quirky touches included alien-looking metal mannequins and TV monitors embedded into the floor, which played his fashion shows.

His Paris store on rue Vivienne backed onto Galerie Vivienne, the corridor of shops and cafés where Gaultier presented several shows, including his infamous "Chic Rabbis" collection. The location of the London store was at the heart of the revitalized Brompton Cross shopping district, which also included a store and restaurant fronted by retailer Joseph Ettedgui, the lavish Conran Shop situated in the historic Michelin House, and the vast, warehouse-like Katharine Hamnett flagship store designed by Norman Foster.

Show
Store opening

Date/Time
11th November 1991
6–9pm

Place
171–175 Draycott Avenue
London

Format/Size
Metal, plastic
12.5cm x 10cm
(5in x 4in)

Martin Brading

PX
CLOTHING
29 James Street
Covent Garden
London WC2
Tel 01·240 2527

PX

Show
Promotional material

Date/Time
circa 1978

Place
29 James Street
London

Format/Size
Card
14.5cm x 9cm
(5¾in x 3½in)

During the late 1970s a new group of avant-garde stylists emerged on the London fashion scene. These outrageous individuals later formed the nucleus for what became known as the New Romantics. The utilitarian-looking PX boutique, located in the Covent Garden district of the capital, became a focus for these young people who would hang out in the store with the assistants, Julia Fodor (who later transformed into style-icon "Princess Julia") and Welsh electro pop singer Steve Strange, who would mastermind the notorious Blitz nightclub. Strange and Fodor modelled the designs of storeowners Helen Robinson and Steph Raynor, which were a mix of Germanic army surplus, zig-zag futuristic sportswear and retro-Hollywood glamour. Vintage diamante brooches and medals were big sellers.

PX's high-tech look changed when it moved to Endell Street, Covent Garden. Here, the mood became more flamboyant with a mix of swashbuckling frilly blouses, satin gowns, Little Lord Fauntleroy velvet knickerbocker suits and, later, Hobo cowboys and colourful geishas.

Bastet

Although punk dominated the late 1970s with confrontational clothing that matched the angry soundtrack of the Sex Pistols and The Clash, another equally thought-provoking look was energizing the fashion industry. Designers such as Thierry Mugler in Paris and Antony Price in London were cultivating a futuristic landscape inhabited by space-age sirens in glossy second-skin frocks and would-be Flash Gordons in spiky tailored suits. At Price's Plaza store on the King's Road, London, you ordered clothes through a hatch like fast food.

The future had also arrived in Knightsbridge, where Bastet, a German former model named after the ancient Egyptian cat-goddess, opened a shiny emporium filled with tubular black and silver furniture, mosaic mirrors and giant metal Arum lilies either side of the entrance (pictured on this promotional flyer). Her ultra-glamorous, ultra-modern designs were advertised with the tag line: "The Spirit of Utopia Lives". Bastet presented her goddess dresses alongside emerging labels, including RIOT by Paul Dart.

Show
Promotional material

Date/Time
circa 1979

Place
99 Old Brompton Road
London

Format/Size
Paper
19cm x 29.5cm
(7½in x 11½in)

Alexander McQueen

Show
Store opening

Date/Time
4th November 1999
6.30–8.30pm

Place
47 Conduit Street
London

Format/Size
Card
14.5cm x 22.5cm
(5¾in x 8¾in)

For the much-hyped opening of his flagship store in a Grade II listed building in London's smart Mayfair district, Alexander McQueen continued his delightfully contrary behaviour in mailing out an invitation depicting a steamy night-time image of 49th Street in New York, renowned for its porn theatres. The photograph features the World Theater, the cinema that in 1972 found itself at the centre of a scandal when it presented the world premiere of the notorious *Deep Throat*. Rebranded The Embassy in 1982, it opened with a Walt Disney film. McQueen's store was designed by Azman Architects and its stark steel-and-glass interior presented an almost glacial feel that acted as the perfect backdrop for the designer's Autumn/Winter 1999 collection, "The Outlook", based around the 1980 horror movie, *The Shining*. At the time of opening the interior included a gigantic glass display case that sliced through the front window façade and contained a snowstorm tableau, as featured in his show.

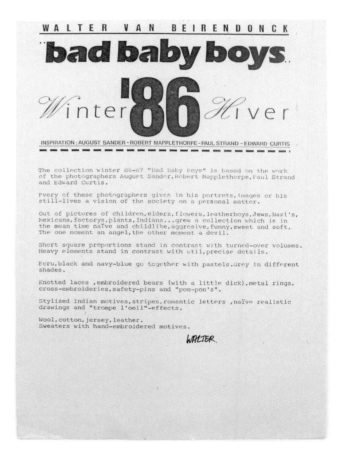

Walter Van Beirendonck

Another designer who was a member of the Antwerp Six, this was the first lavish press pack that idiosyncratic Van Beirendonck mailed to the UK style press in London. His collection continued to express his niche aesthetic that combined homoerotic overtones with a sense of the absurd. The title of this menswear collection, "Bad Baby Boys", was equally provocative as Van Beirendonck dressed strapping male models in pastel coloured sweaters patterned with teddy bears, jersey shorts and leather harness tooled with nursery-style illustrations. The designer cited a list of photographers as his inspiration: August Sander, Robert Mapplethorpe, Paul Strand and Edward Curtis. As with other Belgian designers, Van Beirendonck offered a comprehensive and polished package with high production values, from the top-class imagery to the thoughtfully considered materials. It was immediately noted by the global press, who embraced the new Belgian school of designers and heaped them with praise.

Show
Menswear
Autumn/Winter
1986–87

Date/Time
March 1986

Place
Olympia
Hammersmith Road
London

Format/Size
Paper
29.5cm x 21cm
(11½in x 8¼in)

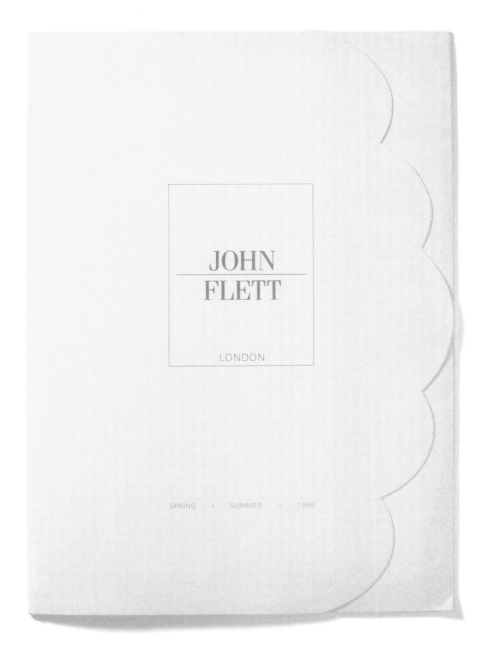

John Flett

Designer John Flett's promotional press pack featuring a scallop-edged cover highlighted one of the main stylistic motifs of his collection. "John develops his signature circular cut from scalloped shells of dresses and jackets that curve around the body," read the press release. "The collection is the essence of femininity." Bows were big with Flett this season, on both his male and female models. Silhouettes fell from broad shoulders to the narrowest of torsos, while trousers abbreviated above the ankle or softly draped over the foot.

Flett's designs flirted with the androgynous mood that pervaded London clubland, with Tanel Bedrossiantz, longtime muse of Jean Paul Gaultier, modelling his menswear in stylish poses more akin to a 1950s mannequin. This elegant attitude was also evident in the womenswear, with décolletage necklines, corseted tailoring and diaphanous details. Flett's name, printed in a soft dove grey on custard yellow, also highlighted the designer's chosen palette: an array of chalky pastels – powder blue, vanilla, dusty lilac, sage and grey – worked with black and midnight.

Show
Press pack
Spring/Summer
1988

Date/Time
October 1987

Place
Marysia Woroniecka PR
Flood Street
London

Format/Size
Card
29.5cm x 21cm
(11¾in x 8¼in)

SUMMER '88

ANN DEMEULEMEESTER

door
PATRICK ROBYN

Ann Demeulemeester

One of the original Antwerp Six, ex-students of the Antwerp Academy who banded together to show at London Fashion Week in 1986, Demeulemeester has always had a penchant for dark romantic imagery. Nowhere was this more evident than in her humble look book that she transformed with her neo-gothic aesthetic from a functional tool into an artistic endeavour, which was art directed by the designer's husband, photographer Patrick Robyn. The graphic design erred on the minimalist, including a title page that luxuriates in an expanse of white space and small-scale font, followed by an updated old master portrait collaged with a mysterious anonymity strip covering the eyes. Wistful black-and-white photographs (by Robyn) allude to the works of painters of the Dutch Golden Age and also reference the 1950 film, *La Beauté du Diable*, that shared the title with the collection. The clothes throughout were long and sombre, capturing the new, understated mood being offered by Demeulemeester and her Belgian counterparts.

Show
Promotional material
Spring/Summer
1988

Date/Time
October 1987

Place
London

Format/Size
Card
24cm x 34cm
(9½in x 13½in)

The text visible on the press pack image:

JOHN GALLIANO

DIRECTOR JOHN GALLIANO ASSISTANT DIRECTOR
AMANDA GRIEVE PHOTOGRAPHER CARRIE BRANOVAN
GRAPHICS CHRISTOPHER WADDEN CO-ORDINATOR
JINA JAY MODEL APPLE HAIR JULIAN L
MAKE-UP ELLIE LOCATION GWYNEDD, NORTH

AUTUMN · WINTER 87·8

A ● W

8 8

JOHN GALLIANO

AGUECHEEK LTD 15 G

Show
Press pack
Autumn/Winter
1987–88

Date/Time
15th March 1987
4pm

Place
British Fashion Council Marquee
Olympia
Hammersmith Road
London

Format/Size
Cardboard box, acetate, fabric
29cm x 29cm
(11¼in x 11¼in)

John Galliano

The illustrated invitation for this show was an extension of the series of images included in this boxed promotional press pack, along with a set of postcards and a giant muslin scarf printed with photographs by Carrie Branovan, styled by Amanda Grieve (now Harlech). By this period in his career, with the financial backing of Aguecheek Galliano had the opportunity to offer a complete image – this package is even decorated with his newly formed heraldic-style coat of arms. This collection was Galliano showcasing his romantic bent – using flowers as inspiration, modelled by a diminutive ingénue called Apple. "Consider the Lilies," asks Galliano. Consider the dresses that explode in an exquisite bouquet or a skirt tailored into a hemline of fallen petals. Again, the look was painstakingly realized from top to toe, from the carefully coiled and pinned hairstyles to the over-the-knee stockings. This was Galliano at his most fragile, delicate and romantic.

Handwritten note on tag:
John Galliano
Autumn Winter 94–95
6 Rue Ferou
75006 Paris
Saturday 05 March 9ʰ 30

John Galliano

The early Saturday morning start was not going to keep those lucky enough to have received John Galliano's rusty key invitation from attending. There had been much talk in advance of the show as the designer faced his latest financial crisis and it was only at the eleventh hour that US *Vogue* editor Anna Wintour and her associate André Leon Talley had persuaded Parisian socialite Sao Schlumberger to allow the designer to stage his presentation in her vacant tumbledown townhouse. Wintour also introduced Galliano to a new backer. A host of supermodels, who walked for free, weaved through a rabbit warren of rooms as journalists sat knee-to-knee on a raggle-taggle of chairs and the odd chaise longue, which also provided the perfect resting place for the weary mannequins. The look was quasi-Oriental, crafted from a few bolts of black and pink fabric. Abbreviated kimonos, svelte tailored jackets or a shrug of a sheepskin falling off the shoulder were secured with a silk obi belt exploding from the back. Each model sported an up-do hairstyle, topped off with a hat that was part Pompidou Centre, part Geisha.

Show
Autumn/Winter
1994–95

Date/Time
5th March 1994
9.30am

Place
6 rue Férou
Paris

Format/Size
Key

On the key tags:

Iain R Webb
alla sfilata A/I 03-04

MOSCHINO
CHEAPANDCHIC
invita

4 marzo 2003 ore 12.30
via Bezzecca, 5
settore B posto 20

Moschino Cheap and Chic

Show
Autumn/Winter
2003–4

Time/Date
4th March 2003
12.30pm

Place
Via Bezzecca, 5
Milan

Format/Size
Set of keys

Since Franco Moschino's death in 1994, the creative team of the label, headed by Rossella Jardini, has done everything to keep the designer's sense of humour alive. This might mean models choreographed to take a dramatic tumble on the catwalk or accessorizing a smart military coat with an authentic busby, as with this show. The invitation to a Moschino show is often where the fun starts, like this set of multicoloured keys, which reappeared during the show dangling from nylon and metal work belts that also held spanners, sunglasses and hairbrushes. The theme was utilitarian chic and featured boyish boiler suits alongside cute tweed skirt suits and fluorescent harnesses worn over fake fur coats. For several seasons, Cheap and Chic shows were staged in the anonymous concrete Milan location of the Aeffe Group, which owns Moschino, in Via Bezzecca. However, the mood of the front row is always lifted by the colourful, crazy antics that appear on the catwalk.

Joseph

This blatantly sexual illustration is by Michael Roberts, who collaborated with retailer Joseph Ettedgui to develop and promote the fashion and lifestyle brand. Roberts is one of fashion's true mavericks. A fashion editor par excellence, photographer and illustrator, his wit earned him notoriety at *The Sunday Times* in the 1970s, while his pastiche fashion stories for *Tatler* were equally tongue-in-chic. The pair were well suited since the retailer was equally nonconformist, as demonstrated by his decision to stage catwalk shows during London Fashion Week. Joseph shows were always a riot, and not just of colour and texture. Audiences went wild for the sexy, homoerotic antics that also featured in the retailer's advertising campaigns (also conceived by Roberts).

For previous shows, Roberts styled Ettedgui's trademark knits with Hawaiian grass skirts and angel wings (on male models), while this particular show opened with model Sharon Dolphin lip-syncing to Diana Ross's "Chain Reaction" and ended with a gaggle of male Dusty Springfield impersonators with tear-stained, blackened eyes.

Show
Autumn/Winter
1986–87

Date/Time
16th March 1986
3.30pm

Place
Duke of York Barracks
King's Road
London

Format/Size
Card
21cm x 15cm
(8¼in x 6in)

Meadham Kirchhoff

Edward Meadham and Benjamin Kirchhoff met while studying at London's Central Saint Martins. The pair quickly became the poster boys of London Fashion Week, their shows becoming a must-see event that had press and buyers fighting fashion student fans to get in.

The duo create an elaborate world starting with multi-layered invitations and show notes, such as this saucy pin-up. This show, presented in the cavernous venue, illustrated just why the designers are such a hot ticket, from the set (arches of pastel balloons and gold tinsel drapes) to the supporting cast of trashy lookalike Courtney Loves, who vamped their way through a can-can as models paraded around them. If that was not enough, the show also featured a gaggle of little girl ballerinas, who twirled (one on top of a cake musical box) to the theme tune from *Edward Scissorhands*. The clothes were equally camp, with rainbow-coloured offerings including cartoony sweaters, baroque party frocks and see-through négligées.

Show
Spring/Summer
2012

Date/Time
20th September 2011
2pm

Place
Old Eurostar Terminal
Waterloo Station
London

Format/Size
Paper
29.5cm x 21cm
(11½in x 8½in)

Jean Paul Gaultier

Despite the saucy invitation, this collection was a pretty buttoned-up affair, with heavily layered outdoorsy outfits featuring polo-neck sweaters, swaggering overcoats and bobble hats. The theme was Eurovision, with the designer taking specific inspiration from Nordic and Bavarian national costume. Models, including Nadja Auermann, Veronica Webb and Christy Turlington, wore long braids that were part-Heidi, part-Pippi Longstocking. Beaded Norwegian sweaters became corsets, brassières and tiny shrugs worn over shirts. Alongside folkloric embroidery decorating deconstructed lederhosen, Gaultier added photographic prints featuring a montage of portraits including his own. Model John Francis wore a polo neck pictured with a naked torso (as seen on the 3D invitation).

For the finale, elaborate headpieces incorporated sunglasses, a pistol, knitting needles (with knitting attached), cigarette holders, ashtrays and a crystal ball. Gaultier's bride, wearing an Aran knit dress, wore a headdress fashioned from toilet-roll holders. As the designer took his final bows, he was almost upstaged by a one-man band's firework display!

Show
Autumn/Winter
1992–93

Date/Time
20th March 1992
6pm

Place
Salle Japy
rue François de Neufchâteau
Paris

Format/Size
Holographic card
12cm x 24cm
(4¾in x 9½in)

Proudly invites you to
The Succubus after party

Basso & Brooke

In 2004 Bruno Basso and Christopher Brooke were the inaugural winners of Fashion Fringe, a design competition focused around London Fashion Week that was the brainchild of the veteran fashion writer Colin McDowell. The panel of judges, which also included British *Vogue* editor Alexandra Shulman and Burberry's CEO Rosemary Bravo, were impressed with the duo's exuberant digital prints that mimicked classic Sloane Ranger headscarves but on closer inspection revealed an "orgiastic carnival of sexual liberation and allegories of power". Basso & Brooke's debut show at London Fashion Week was titled "The Succubus And Other Stories". Staged in the BMW car showroom in South West London, the pair's notoriety ensured it was standing room only. This collection was no less powerful with equally fantastical prints layered one upon another to riotous effect. The duo certainly had reason to celebrate at their after-party. In 2009, Basso & Brooke made headlines when US First Lady Michele Obama wore one of their designs for an "Evening of Poetry and the Spoken Word" at the White House.

Show
Autumn/Winter
2005–6

Date/Time
13th February 2005
3.30pm

Place
BMW Westminster
78–98 Marsham Street
London

Format/Size
Card
21cm x 15cm
(8¼in x 5¾in)

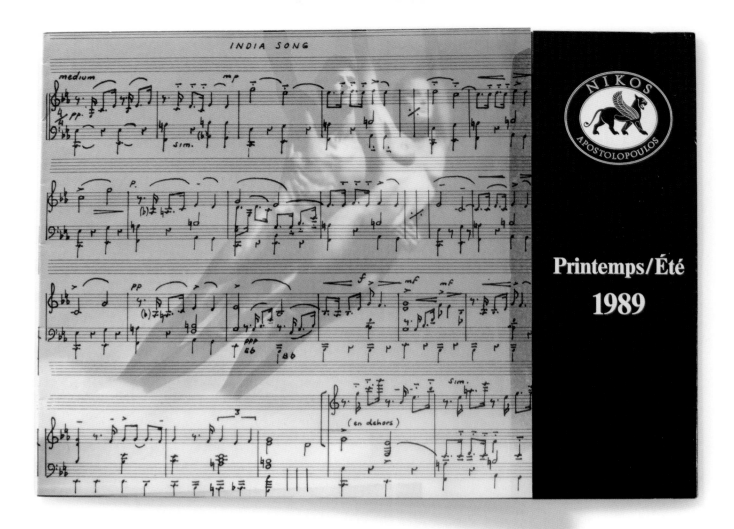

INDIA SONG

Nikos

Show
Spring/Summer
1989

Date/Time
October 1988

Place
Paris

Format/Size
Card, acetate
21cm x 30cm
(8¼in x 11¾in)

The images of athletic models posing naked in a puff of ethereal clouds encapsulated the spiritual mood of the designer this season. This was highlighted by the accompanying text by Hermann Hesse referencing *Siddharta*, a novel that deals with a journey of self-discovery. Nikos Apostolopoulos enjoys taking his audience on a dramatic adventure and his shows became a must-see event, not least because of the designer's penchant for half-naked, hard-bodied models. In the world of Nikos shoulders are broad and muscles supertoned, a look epitomized by blond Adonis Steve Lyon. The designer's pursuit of perfection is hard-wired in his Greek heritage, reaching back to Aristotle.

In this show Nikos appeared to take inspiration from theatrical and cinematic favourites set against a soundtrack of rousing theme tunes. A 1950s *West Side Story* tableau merged with *Gone With The Wind* and then a scene from a would-be Tennessee Williams play. One moment the models were kitted out in ivory tuxedos, the next posing heroically in second-skin underwear.

22/09/09

Nasir Mazhar

At this womenswear accessories presentation Nasir Mazhar continued to offer a combination of hi-gloss pin-up girls (think illustrator Alberto Vargas) and hard-edged glamazons (think street-wise sirens). Mazhar was born in London's East End and his work reflects the reality and swagger of the urban grime music scene. This collection featured flamboyant "NM" initial knuckleduster rings, long gold curlicue fingernails and a giant tartan, taffeta hair-bow hat.

Having originally trained as a hairdresser, Mazhar launched his career as a milliner. His style is unashamedly theatrical so it is not surprising that the designer has worked on productions at the Royal Opera House, The National, the Rambert Dance Company, as well as Kylie Minogue's "Showgirl" tour of 2005. He has also collaborated with London designers, including Gareth Pugh, Louise Gray and Meadham Kirchhoff. In 2011 Mazhar launched his womenswear line, followed by menswear the following season. He has quickly developed a cult following who love his humorous cartoony style and devil-may-care attitude.

Show
Spring/Summer
2010

Date/Time
22nd September 2009
4–5pm

Place
The Vault
Somerset House
The Strand
London

Format/Size
Card
21cm x 14.5cm
(8¼in x 5¾in)

Guys ♥ B.J.
BETSEY JOHNSON SPRING '04.

Monday September 15th, 2003
4:00 pm   The Gertrude at Bryant Park
R.S.V.P. 212-625-1000 ext. 55

SECTION   ROW   SEAT

Show
Spring/Summer
2004

Date/Time
15th September 2003
4pm

Place
Gertrude Pavilion
Bryant Park
New York

Format/Size
Card, sticker
7cm x 23.5cm
(3in x 9¼in)

Betsey Johnson

For this show the septuagenarian Mother of American Pop Fashion presented a supper club vibe, with guests sitting at tables and drinks being served. Betsey Johnson was in a fizzy mood (literally) as models dressed in frothy, barely-there approximations of French maids' outfits carried magnum bottles of Taittinger champagne, presumably to placate a sponsor. From there the collection bubbled with the usual Johnson fare that included skimpy cropped tops decorated with flirty feathers, tighter-than-tight jeans, overflowing corsets and micro-miniskirts and dresses. The designer added a Puerto Rico via New Jersey vibe with topless Latino boys in pin-stripe trousers, wife-beater vests, gold jewellery (and teeth) and tattoos. Johnson delighted in the naughty ambience from the show's double entendre title to the glittery nipple tassels that looked like souvenirs of a cross-border spring-break trip. And right down to the finale, where six Lolita-lookalike models lifted their nighties to reveal "BYE BYE" printed on their panties.

Issey Miyake

The choice of venue for the Issey
Miyake show, the Museum of Modern
Art in Paris, couldn't have been
more appropriate for a designer
who has spent his entire career
trying to capture the moment when
fashion and art collide. Invariably,
on the Miyake catwalk, the two
mediums co-exist. This season was
no different, with his protégé, the
label's incumbent designer Naoki
Takizawa, presenting a collection
that mixed the arty with the artificial,
the elegant with the experimental. In
something of a tradition for the label,
one segment of the show featured
models on the catwalk unzipping
hooded space-age jumpsuits to reveal
second-skin bodysuits covered with
what resembled the tattoo markings
of some futuristic tribe. These patterns
were scaled up giant size on the
metallic sculptural backdrop for
the show and were the very same
ones that featured on the somewhat
risqué "Mona Lisa" invitation and
programme, painted by graphic artist
Tadanori Yokoo.

Show
Spring/Summer
2004

Date/Time
8th October 2003
8.30pm

Place
Musée d'Art Moderne de la Ville
de Paris
11 avenue du Président Wilson
Paris

Format/Size
Card
26cm x 18cm
(10in x 7¼in)

ISSEY MIYAKE
BY NAOKI TAKIZAWA

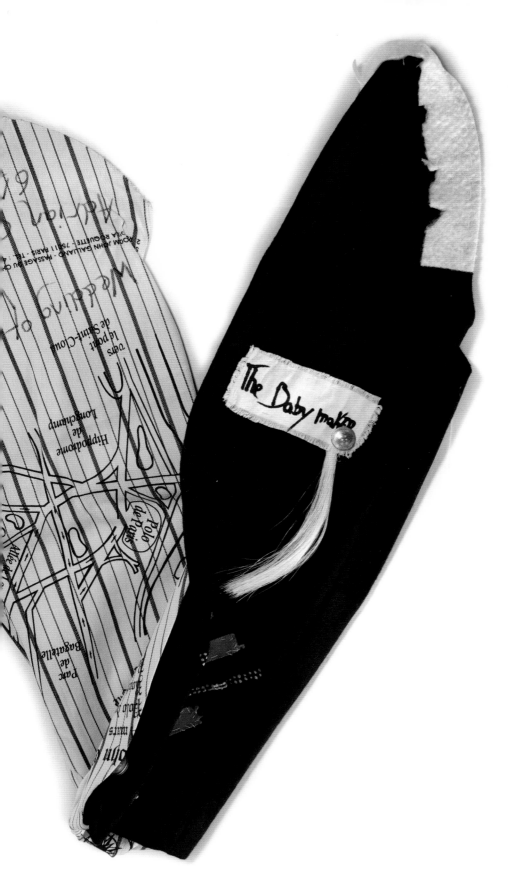

John Galliano

This show opened to the sound of thundering buffalo hooves while a handsome stallion and equally striking rider performed tricks in the sand-covered set decorated with naive paintings and mystical assemblages of rocks, wood, oil drums, tyres and animal bones. The show mixed nineteenth-century Civil War uniforms, Little House On the Prairie underpinnings, Native American costume and 1950s couture via Alfred Hitchcock with The Osmonds singing "Crazy Horses". Models, including Shalom Harlow (a Galliano favourite), Chandra North, Kylie Bax and Kate Moss, wore elaborate spiky Mohawk hairstyles adorned with multiple metal clips and tribal face paint. They were wrapped in blanket coats appliquéd with folkloric patterns, slashed Cavalry jackets, billowing plaid gowns and little black suits with arrowhead lace trims. A black ruffled finale gown was accessorized with an eagle headpiece made entirely of wooden ice-lolly sticks by milliner Stephen Jones.

This invitation featured a naively decorated sleeve ripped from a Civil War military jacket.

Show
Autumn/Winter
1996–97

Date/Time
14 March 1996
7.30pm

Place
Polo de Paris
Route des Moulins
Paris

Format/Size
Jacket sleeve
122cm x 20cm
(48in x 8in)

Margaret Howell

Tradition is at the heart of Margaret Howell's brand so it is not surprising that, combined with the relaxed attitude inherent in her designs, this should inform her minimal catwalk presentations. Season after season, journalists head for her central London store, where they find the same set-up: a sparse white catwalk, barely a foot high, set against the white back wall of the store. On either side are two rows of white benches. Front-row regulars know exactly where to find their place on the seating plan. It is this familiarity that is central to Howell's design ethos, with outfits on the runway constructed with items that feel as if they already belong in your wardrobe but given a subtle update. These are inevitably cut from quality, natural fabrics – cotton, leather, silk and tweed – a swatch of which is pictured on the functional invitation. Howell's love of fine, unerring design quality means that, usually, the store is not only filled with garments of her own design but also things that she is drawn to, whether Ercol furniture, Robert Welch stainless-steel cutlery or Anglepoise lamps.

Show
Autumn/Winter
2008–9

Date/Time
14th February 2008
1.15pm

Place
Margaret Howell
34 Wigmore Street
London

Format/Size
Card
21cm x 15cm
(8¼in x 6in)

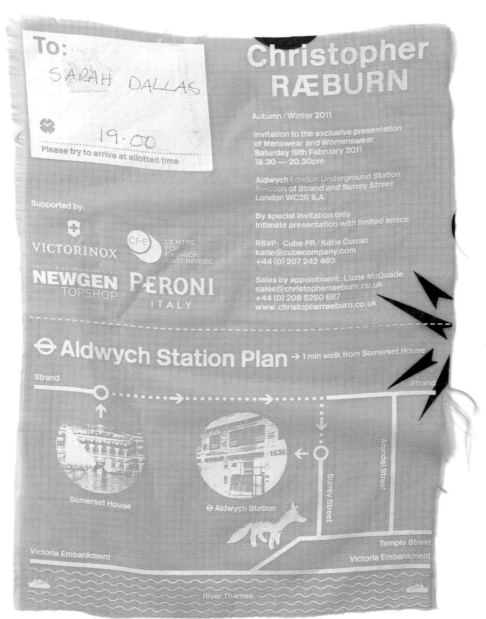

TO:
SARAH DALLAS

19.00
Please try to arrive at allotted time

Supported by:

VICTORINOX

NEWGEN
TOPSHOP

CFE CENTRE FOR FASHION ENTERPRISE

PERONI
ITALY

Christopher RÆBURN

Autumn/Winter 2011

Invitation to the exclusive presentation of Menswear and Womenswear
Saturday 19th February 2011
18.30 — 20.30pm

Aldwych London Underground Station
Junction of Strand and Surrey Street
London WC2R 1LA

By special invitation only
Intimate presentation with limited space

RSVP: Cube PR / Katie Curran
katie@cubecompany.com
+44 (0) 207 242 483

Sales by appointment: Lizzie McQuade
sales@christopherraeburn.co.uk
+44 (0) 208 5250 687
www.christopherraeburn.co.uk

⊖ Aldwych Station Plan → 1 min walk from Somerset House

Strand
Strand
Somerset House
⊖ Aldwych Station
Arundel Street
Surrey Street
Temple Street
Victoria Embankment
Victoria Embankment
River Thames

Christopher Raeburn

Christopher Raeburn graduated from London's Royal College of Art in 2006, where he studied womenswear. However, the designer's functional urban style has a unisex appeal and he is now equally acclaimed as a menswear designer. In 2011 Raeburn won the Emerging Talent Menswear award at the British Fashion Awards. He gained attention for outwear created from de-commissioned parachutes (also used for this invitation), and this re-made concept is now central to his brand.

This particular presentation showcased his collection called Blast with typical ingenuity: giant inflatable animals were placed around the disused underground station, while his models posed in redundant phone booths before wandering through the booking hall, watched by guests who stood around as if waiting for news of a cancelled train. Raeburn's girls wore peaked visors and strappy platform sandals, while his boys donned tough Dr. Marten boots. Both modelled grey leggings teamed with military-style hooded jackets and coats in shades of grey, khaki, silver, mauve and orange.

Show
Autumn/Winter
2011–12

Date/Time
19th February 2011
6.30–8.30pm

Place
Aldwych Underground Station
London

Format/Size
Parachute fabric
29cm x 20.5cm
(11½in x 8in)

Lainey Keogh

Around this period The Cobden Working Mens Club became a trendy location for creative Londoners. While the clientele indulged in a game of pool and a pint, the atmosphere was unpretentious bordering on the crude. The interior's rundown appearance certainly suited Irish designer Keogh's gauzy knits with trailing threads and unravelling hems. For the show several members of the invited audience were conspicuously positioned on a raised stage area, almost becoming part of the action as models paraded past.

Keogh's organic-looking designs were knitted in the rich and full-bodied shades featured on the invitation, including beetroot red, moss green and slate grey. These were modelled by a line-up of stellar models including Linda Evangelista, Naomi Campbell, Jodie Kidd, Honor Fraser and Helena Christensen, each sporting a tumbling Rapunzel-like hairstyle intertwined with twigs and leaves. The show also featured the modelling debut of a voluptuous alabaster-skinned Sophie Dahl in a see-through metallic baby-doll dress. The soundtrack included unreleased U2 tracks and actor John Hurt reciting poetry by Ireland's Seamus Heaney.

Show
Autumn/Winter
1997–98

Date/Time
24th February 1997
3.45pm

Place
The Cobden Working Mens Club
170–172 Kensal Road
London

Format/Size
Paper, fabric
21cm x 13.5cm
8¼in x 5½in)

Dolce & Gabbana

Although the label on this fabric swatch invitation stated "Made in Italy", this season Domenico Dolce and Stefano Gabbana cast their ideal man as a heritage hybrid of Sicilian peasant and North of England docker, circa 1940, played out to an Ennio Morricone soundtrack. Brawny models wore soft woollen donkey jackets, thick-knit sweaters (sometimes sleeveless over a rumpled T-shirt) and wide flannel pants. They were accessorized with cosy scarves, snug beanie hats and, oddly for an Autumn/Winter collection, open-toed sandals. Layering various shades of grey – from charcoal to dove, tone on tone – the collection was an exploration of textures, highlighted by the addition of shiny black PVC or fancy embroidery on a boxy wool jacket.

The show was presented in the design duo's glamorous new showrooms, with red-carpeted staircase and blackened marble floors. Dolce & Gabbana always open their shows with Pietro Mascagni's evocative "Cavalleria Rusticana – Intermezzo", as featured in the opening credits of the film *Raging Bull*.

Show
Menswear
Autumn/Winter
1998–99

Date/Time
11th January 1998
1pm

Place
Via San Damiano, 9
Milan

Format/Size
Paper, fabric
21.5cm x 14.5cm
(8½in x 5¾in)

Willi Smith/WilliWear

Even when Willi Smith's designs appeared to be ultra classic (the designer even called one collection "Totally Classic"), they were always given some kind of funky twist. His work was imbued with fun and he cultivated a wacky cartoon style that played with proportion. "[My clothes] must have a sense of humour," he said. Smith also embraced the art world. He was attracted by the freedom enjoyed by artists: "Designers have the clothing disease, that's just all we talk about, but artists do what comes from within." For this project he commissioned a group of disparate contemporary artists to design an image to be reproduced on T-shirts, among them Gilbert & George, Paula Rego and Derek Jarman. In 1983 Smith collaborated with sculptor Christo to produce another T-shirt for his "Surrounded Islands" project in Florida. This collection of postcards was packaged to promote the Artist T-shirt project, and included printed information highlighting Smith's upcoming showings at both mens- and womenswear shows in London.

Show
Autumn/Winter
1988–89

Date/Time
12th–15th March 1988

Place
British Designer Show
Olympia 2
Hammersmith Road
London

Format/Size
Envelope containing postcards
15cm x 10cm
(6in x 4in)

Saint Laurent

Saint Laurent designer Hedi Slimane loves a bit of teenage rampage and this collection showcased the skinny silhouette and swagger of Fifties rockabilly mimicked in the Eighties with a nod to the seminal output of Malcolm McLaren and Vivienne Westwood in the "Let it Rock" incarnation of their King's Road clothing emporium, c.1972. On the catwalk that meant winklepicker shoes, greased-back hair and leather pants – this time around less Jim Morrison, more Dave Gahan of Depeche Mode. Slimane's shows are layered with references. This season's invitation, packaged as a pocket-diary sized book, featured abstract artist Matt Connors, his latest culture crush. Slimane is a big fan of art and music and understands the desire for associated ephemera; this booklet has already become collectable. The designer's vision reaches beyond the catwalk and the clothes; it is also found in the photographs he takes, his subjects (usually punky rock'n'rollers or angsty teens) and the worlds they inhabit.

Show
Menswear
Spring/Summer
2014

Date/Time
30th June 2013
8pm

Place
Grand Palais
3 avenue du Général Eisenhower
Paris

Format/Size
Booklet
20cm x 30cm
(8in x 12in)

Show
Autumn/Winter
2010–11

Date/Time
22nd February 2010
7.30pm

Place
Serpentine Gallery
Kensington Gardens
London

Format/Size
Tote bag
34cm x 43cm
(13½in x 17in)

Pringle of Scotland

An art theme ran through this Pringle of Scotland presentation from the choice of gallery venue to the invitation, which featured an artwork by Stephen Sutcliffe depicting a deconstructed Argyle pattern in grey and white reminiscent of the Scottish architect, designer and artist Charles Rennie Mackintosh, and the complementary tote bag illustrated by David Shrigley.

To celebrate the founding of the Scottish knitwear label in 1815, the show was used to announce the launch of a collaborative project between Pringle and the Serpentine Gallery in London that involved a group of artists selected to create new works in response to iconic products associated with the label. Along with Shrigley, these included Douglas Gordon, Luke Fowler, Richard Wright, Jim Lambie and Tilda Swinton, who had become the face of the brand, appearing in the advertising campaigns. Swinton sat front row with the photographer Ryan McGinley and singer Janet Jackson. Shrigley also made a short animated film titled *The Jumper*, which was screened at menswear collections A/W 2010 in Milan.

Jean Muir

The invitation features an oil painting, *Jean Muir Checking Buttons* (1979), by the English artist Anthony Green. Perhaps what drew Miss Muir to Green was his use of irregularly shaped canvases that resemble the complex pattern pieces required to construct her seemingly effortless designs. Muir enjoyed the mathematics of pattern cutting and always somewhat self-effacingly referred to herself as a "dressmaker". The designer consistently eschewed the brouhaha of the flamboyant catwalk show and instead presented superbly edited collections from her tiny showroom in London's West End (depicted on the invitation) on just a handful of models.

Season after season she followed this pattern, no matter the ever-changing styles or hemlines. Models were made up in the same fashion (neat hair, red lips) and paraded under the twinkling chandelier to tapes compiled of Muir's favourite piano or jazz music. This intimate environment was totally in tune with the understated vision of Muir's fashion, which, this season, included ensembles fashioned from tobacco suede, creamy angora knit and pearlized leather.

Show
Autumn/Winter
1988–89

Date/Time
13th March 1988
9.45pm

Place
Jean Muir Showroom
22 Bruton Street
London

Format/Size
Card
14.5cm x 10cm
(5¾in x 4in)

Show
Spring/Summer
2006

Giles

Date/Time
18th September 2005
7.30pm

Place
Freemasons' Hall
Great Queen Street
London

Format/Size
Card
15cm x 21cm
(5¾ x 8¼in)

The invitation features the 1963 painting *Two Waiting Women and B-58 Nuclear Bomber* by artist Colin Self, depicting two smartly turned-out women, whose perfect world is interrupted. This disquieting scene set the tone for Giles' collection that was at the same time elegant and sophisticated, yet a bit oddball. From the start of his career, Giles targeted an older, sophisticated client, offering seriously constructed suits and dresses alongside poolside-posing gowns. For this collection, he continued to work with couture-type fabrics, while referencing the soigné stylistic vocabulary of the yesteryear salon show: a waterfall frill, a boned corset, the duster coat and baby-doll dress. When supermodel Jade Parfitt appeared wearing a long, strapless gown, she looked a dead ringer for actress Helen Mirren, who is, no doubt, the designer's perfect customer. The stunning interior of the Freemasons' Hall in London was yet another reminder of the extraordinary venues that invitation-only guests are privileged to witness.

Roksanda Ilincic

Serbian Roksanda Ilincic first appeared on the London fashion scene in 2002 when she founded her label after graduating from the MA Fashion course at London's Central Saint Martins. A Snow White beauty that exudes the kind of modern elegance her haute ready-to-wear designs deserve, the one-time model is the best advertisement for her label. For this polite breakfast show (her debut on the schedule at London Fashion Week) she chose Sir Terence Conran's Bibendum restaurant, with guests sat at tables munching croissants and sipping coffee. She showed only a dozen looks. Ilincic's menu offered a taste of yesteryear – voluminous silhouettes with pouffed skirts, cabbage rose prints and embroideries and a haze of tulle or roughly pleated drapery in fondant satin. "I do enjoy dressing up," said the designer, who took her bow in a crimson frock featuring more roses. The look has proved a winner and she is immensely popular with elegant women of style, such as actress Emily Blunt and Catherine, Duchess of Cambridge.

Show
Spring/Summer
2006

Date/Time
20th September 2005
Breakfast

Place
Bibendum Restaurant
Michelin House
81 Fulham Road
London

Format/Size
Paper
29.5cm x 21cm
(11½in x 8¼in)

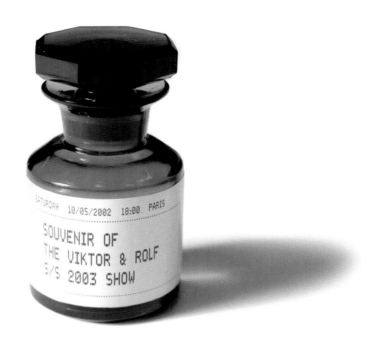

Viktor & Rolf

Show
Spring/Summer
2003

Date/Time
5th October 2002
6pm

Place
Paris

Format/Size
Glass bottle
5.5cm x 3cm
(2¼in x 1¼in)

This show, called "Flowers", provided the biggest surprise of the season. The ever-inventive Dutch design duo, Viktor Horsting and Rolf Snoeren, decided to leave the conceptualizing at home and throw a disco dance party. With pink champagne flowing and a silver glitter-ball spinning overhead, models enjoyed the opportunity to let their hair down. And the fake hair too, including Rapunzel-style extensions, crimped wedge wigs and candyfloss coloured hairpieces by Eugene Souleiman. The sound system blasted out hits by Michael Jackson, Kylie Minogue, Anita Ward, George Michael and of course, Gloria Gaynor and her anthem, "I Will Survive".

Voluminous dresses, often adorned with tiers of frills, were covered in the kind of floral prints usually found in an upholstery department. British model Erin O'Connor appeared at the end of the show, gyrating in a long coatdress made from multicoloured fake flowers. The designers said their minds had been on their new fragrance. "This is not a fragrance," read the shownotes. "It is a memory... the actual essence of desire... our dreams."

Walter Van Beirendonck

Aware that his tongue-twister name might cause problems, Belgian Van Beirendonck used just his first name. This collection was the designer's reaction to the fitness fad. Instead of trying to squeeze his customers into a Lycra version of perfection, he created a softer silhouette with cuddly, oversized knitwear that actually added extra inches. These sweaters were decorated with flowers and toy animals. Others, embroidered with the words "HUG ME", were worn with strongman leggings, romper-style shorts and tough boots. There were also fleece sweatshirts and trousers printed with more slogans and cartoon furry animals. His choice of more worldly-wise looking male models is also noteworthy. With their twirled moustaches, broken noses and bald heads, they resembled a troupe of turn-of-the-century wrestlers or showmen. Van Beirendonck's vision offered a cosy, indulgent version of men's fashion far from the power-dressed Masters of the Universe of late 1980s Wall Street. As the poster promised, Van Beirendonck was "original and unique".

Show
Menswear
Autumn/Winter
1987–88

Date/Time
14th–17th March 1987

Place
British Designer Show
Olympia 2
Hammersmith Road
London

Format/Size
Poster
55cm x 35.5cm
(22in x 14in)

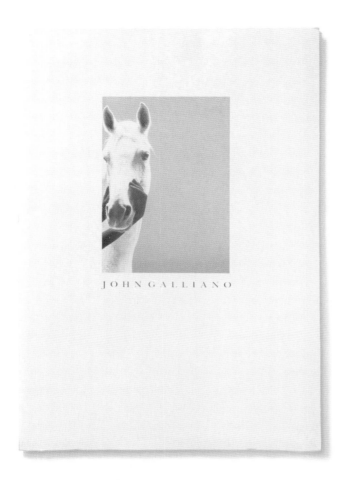

Show
Spring/Summer
1988

Date/Time
11th October 1987
6.30pm

Place
British Fashion Council
Marquee
Olympia 2
Hammersmith Road
London

Format/Size
Card
30cm x 20.5cm
(11¾in x 8in)

John Galliano

This was one of the shows that sealed John Galliano's fate as a designer of serious international note. It was exquisitely finessed from start to finish, from his miraculously tailored designs that seemed to flow around his models to the decidedly elegant styling, hair and make-up. His muse paraded in over-the-elbow opera gloves, pastel tights and pale character dance shoes. Not surprisingly, he was awarded his first Designer of the Year title at this time.

The invitation for the show depicted a historical illustration featuring women in Empire-line costumes, inspired by classical antiquity. Similar engravings were also used to decorate his promotional pack (seen here). Galliano has always been a style magpie, magically mixing different eras and cultures so while the photographs (above) by Carrie Branovan included in the pack allude to a dreamy heroine – part ballet dancer showgirl, part Edwardian lady motorist – other illustrations (not shown) are more contemporary in style, referencing the elegant 1950s fashion drawings of René Gruau, Jean Demarchy and Sigrid Hunt, and explicitly the look of actress Marlene Dietrich.

Press Contact:

Maryshia Woroniecka Publicity.

01-352 7307 & 01-352 3828

Buyers Contact:

Jacquie.

at

John Flett.

3rd Floor, 66-70 Worship Street,

London EC2.

Telephone 01-247 7074.

John Flett

John Flett was among a group of designers who emerged in the shadow of the New Romantic movement with an in-built love of historicism. Models were often styled to resemble bluestocking aesthetes who might befriend Virginia Woolf or Edith Sitwell. For this collection, called "Presenting Gloria", Flett asked David Hiscock, who was creating innovative fashion photography for the style press, to produce promotional pictures. Flett loved Hiscock's purposely-damaged imagery and always chose photographs more defaced than less, even happy to allow Hiscock's scratching technique to encroach on his elegant silhouettes. The photographer remembers a chaotic shoot at Flett's studio in East London, already starting to become an enclave of designers and artists, while PRs such as Marysia Woroniecka were based in West London (Chelsea, Covent Garden and West End). The event was also memorable for Hiscock, as this was the first time he worked with model Isobel Deeley, whom he would go on to date.

Show
Autumn/Winter
1986–87

Date/Time
14th–17th March 1986
9am–6pm

Place
Alexander Studios
Jubilee Place
London

Format/Size
Card
18.5cm x 25cm
(7¼in x 9¾in)

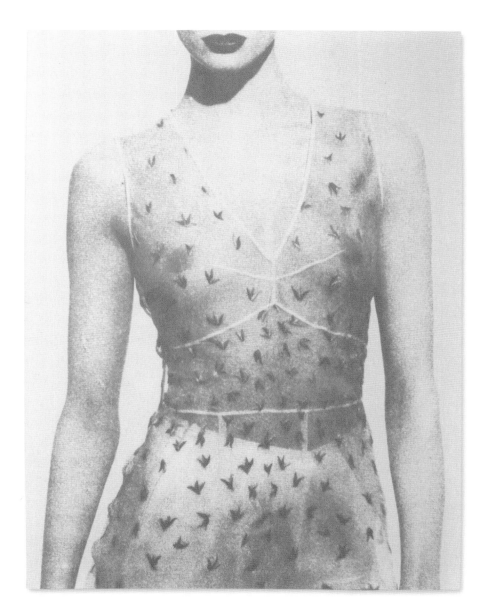

Prada

For this show, the invitation and programme included this image printed in blush pink onto a sheet of acetate. The photograph is by Peter Lindbergh and features model Kristen McMenamy, taken from a series commissioned specifically for the season's accompanying advertising campaign. In these photographs, McMenamy also appears full-length, her startling swept-up strawberry-blonde hairdo in dynamic contrast to her pale complexion. McMenamy's deep red wine lipstick and matching nail polish echoes the only hint of colour in the collection, which was almost entirely milky white, black and silver grey.

The acetate image also reflected the sheer element in Miuccia Prada's collection, affording many of the ensembles a look of yesteryear lingerie. Think Elizabeth Taylor in *Cat On A Hot Tin Roof*. These fragile designs were contrasted with prim, buttoned-up suits. Although this silhouette may have erred on the retro, Prada's love of innovation and offbeat juxtapositions manifested as nylon zips, utilitarian metallic belt buckles and clear plastic mules.

Show
Spring/Summer
1995

Date/Time
6th October 1994
10am

Place
Via Maffei, 2
Milan

Format/Size
Acetate
28.5cm x 22cm
(11½in x 8½in)

Wooyoungmi

South Korean designer Woo Youngmi has built her menswear label along with her sister, Woo Janghee. This collection, which featured 38 looks, was called "The Science of Dress", so it's not surprising that the stylized lookbook, with its graph paper and handwritten information, resembles a scholarly notebook. This also goes to reinforce the image of the Wooyoungmi man, who was presented on the catwalk as a scholarly type, wearing studious-looking half spectacles, jackets with pen-loop pockets and always toting a sleek file case. The finale of the show saw the troop of male models all reappear wearing a trench-cum-lab coat.

The designers favoured a muted palette of blues, greys, browns and greens for their collection that included tie-belt coats with the ease of a dressing gown and eccentric touches such as a wedge shoe with a cutaway peep toe or a pair of shorts that appear to have been merged with a skirt.

Show
Menswear
Spring/Summer
2011

Date/Time
June 2010

Place
Paris

Format/Size
Notebook, elastic
22.5cm x 15.5cm
(8¾in x 6in)

The Fifth Circle

The Fifth Circle was a menswear show featuring designers John Richmond, Destroy, Joe Casely-Hayford, Nick Colman and Duffer of St George, a label comprised of four young men from East London: Barrie Sharpe, Eddie Prendergast, Marco Cairns and Cliff Bowen. The collective's debut was staged in the then-derelict Spitalfields Market, which made a fantastically edgy location, although pigeons proved a problem. The answer? A falcon, to scare them away. The show programmes were a spoof on notebooks used by front row editors – these school-style exercise books not only included show credits but also fashion sketches felt-penned by local school children. The show, which was compèred by Richard Jobson, previously lead singer with the Skids, included Casely-Hayford's twisted jeans, blanket-stitched hipsters and suede and leather safari shirts; Duffer's old-man-style cardigans, reefer jackets and velvet collared coats; Coleman's zipper jackets and shirts and ticking stripe jeans; and Richmond's glittering sequin, beaded and embroidered ensembles.

Show
Menswear
Spring/Summer
1992

Date/Time
1st September 1991
12.30pm

Place
Spitalfields Market
Brushfield Street
London

Format/Size
Notebook
20.5cm x 16.5cm
(8in x 6½in)

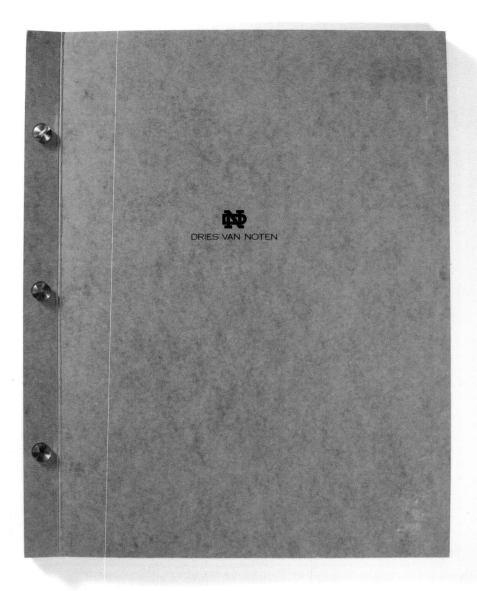

Dries Van Noten

It is often wrongly assumed that the designers who made up the Antwerp Six all shared the same dark, neo-gothic aesthetic air of deconstruction that has become synonymous with, and shorthand for the school of Belgian design. However, this is to misrepresent the original group of designers who actually relished their differences. Dries Van Noten resolutely established his own style from the moment his first model appeared on the London catwalk: a mix of misty-eyed nostalgia and suave elegance with a hint of the comedic. This collection, entitled "Rich Men, Poor Men", continued the designer's love affair with the languid looks of the 1920s and 30s – wine coloured wool stripes, waistcoats and windowpane checks. Again, Van Noten produced a top-quality lookbook that was bolted together with brass screws and includes watermarked trace-paper leaf pages to protect the atmospheric black-and-white photographic prints. There were also pages left blank for the press to make notes.

Show
Autumn/Winter
1987–88

Date/Time
14th–17th March 1987

Place
Olympia 2
Hammersmith Road
London

Format/Size
Notebook
29.5cm x 23cm
(11½in x 9in)

WOMENSWEAR
AUTUMN/WINTER 2013

18 FEBRUARY 2013 4PM
KENSINGTON GARDENS
KENSINGTON GORE
LONDON SW7

ENTRANCE VIA QUEEN'S GATE

AE55

Show
Autumn/Winter
2013–14

Date/Time
18th February 2013
4pm

Place
Kensington Gardens
Kensington Gore
London

Format/Size
Card (unfolded)
21cm x 30cm
(8¼in x 11½in)

Burberry Prorsum

This pop-up London scene was a treatment that chief creative officer Christopher Bailey had previously used for his other showings. This time around, the invitation depicted Burberry HQ and the giant tent erected in Kensington Gardens especially for the show against a backdrop of London's famous tourist sights, including Big Ben and Nelson's Column. Was Bailey suggesting that Burberry was now such an attraction? Certainly, the English capital is at the heart of the brand; there is even a range of iconic pieces called Burberry London.

For this show classic raincoats were cut in rubber, along with pencil skirts that revealed heart print knickers, as Bailey channelled Christine Keeler, the sex-scandal model who embodied London in the Swinging Sixties. That same kinky gloss was applied to cashmere to give the appearance of plastic, while elsewhere, shiny metal highlighted pockets, shoulders and waists. Bailey's aim was to combine the brand's heritage with something a little bit cheeky and naughty. How thoroughly British!

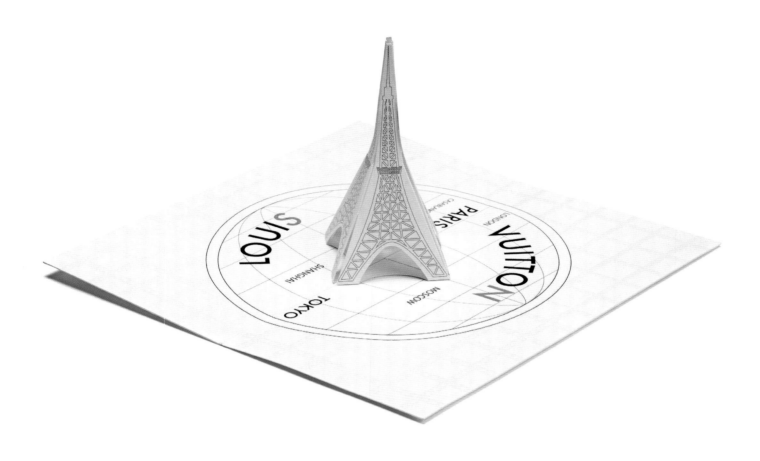

Louis Vuitton

This pop-up invitation clearly stated the theme of the collection as being "a tale of two cities", Paris and Tokyo, which also appeared on the catwalk spelled out (literally) in metallic letters on the models' belts. The catwalk itself featured a massive mirrored sphere, reflected in the silvered arrow pins that pierced jackets and coats and the pointy metallic toecaps of the shoes worn by the slick-looking models. As a brand, Louis Vuitton spells luxury, luxury, luxury and, in his second season as creative director, Kim Jones made the most of the company's extraordinary resource, the team of talented artisans who dream up futuristic fabrics, which they use alongside silk handwoven in Japan. Travel is embedded in the DNA of both Jones and the fashion house, so the collection was a homage to these two diverse cultures. For those who couldn't make it to Paris, the show was beamed live, not from the top of the Eiffel Tower but via the company's website and Facebook page. Totally modern.

Show
Menswear
Autumn/Winter
2012–13

Date/Time
19th January 2012
2.30pm

Place
Serre du parc
André Citroën
2 rue de la Montagne de la Fage
Paris

Format/Size
Card (unfolded)
25.5cm x 25.5cm
(10in x 10in)

"the Family that eats together stays together..."

Show
Autumn/Winter
2007–8

Date/Time
3rd March 2007
8pm

Place
Carreau du Temple
3 rue Dupetit-Thouars
Paris

Format/Size
Card (unfolded)
35cm x 24.5cm
(13½in x 9½in)

John Galliano

Before the show, as the audience of press and buyers watched a grainy black-and-white film of the designer in creation mode, primping models and posing for the camera, a cast of other characters looked on: a deposed duke and duchess, a lusty sailor, a fusty butler and an old woman knitting, as crazy as the dysfunctional family featured on the invitation. In a series of elaborate tableaux, exquisitely staged by set designer Michael Howells, Galliano's extras provided their own backdrop to the collection. And then there were the models who, with blackened eyes and lips and frizzy shocks of hair, looked as though they had just walked from the demi-monde photographs of Brassaï or a painting by Otto Dix.

This presentation marked a return of Galliano as showman. Wearing pyjamas and Wellington boots and carrying a pitchfork, the designer took his bows to an accordion playing "La Vie En Rose". This show had everything, even some live chickens!

Jean Paul Gaultier

As the pop-up Adam and Eve
invitation suggested, this show was set
in an approximation of the Garden
of Eden. There were also shades of
The Blue Lagoon (the 1980 castaway
film starring Brooke Shields and
Christopher Atkins) about the staging;
the turquoise blue catwalk strewn
with flower petals and the backdrop
draped with white parachute silk. Not
surprisingly, the collection featured
both mens- and womenswear,
modelled by Amanda Cazalet and
Stephane Sednaoui (who both
appear on the invitation), Tony Ward,
Cameron Alborzian, Scott Benoit and
the silver-haired Madame Trèmois to a
soundtrack that mixed squawking birds
with dub reggae.

   Matching His'n'Hers looks
juxtaposed suits with detachable
sleeves, jackets with tutu skirts
attached, boys in sarong skirts, girls in
Oxford blue shirts-cum-dresses and a
finale of fishscale sequins, rhinestone
plastic macs and scuba suits, all
topped with dreadlocks and Rasta
man knitted hats. For a final evening
look, a couple shared a dress and
tailcoat joined at the hem.

Show
Spring/Summer
1991

Date/Time
19th October 1990
6pm

Place
Espace Elysée
78 avenue des Champs Elysées
Paris

Format/Size
Card (unfolded)
41cm x 55.5cm
(16in x 21¾in)

J.W. Anderson

The stratospheric rise of young Irish designer Jonathan William Anderson has been astonishing. Launching his menswear label in 2008 and womenswear in 2010, he was immediately tipped as one-to-watch. Press and buyers noted the designer's strong and original handwriting. Such accolades created a buzz around him and ensured a packed house for this show called "The Devoured and I".

Anderson's collection offered an interpretation on the hard and soft theme that juxtaposed hippies and punk rockers: dip-dye and floral prints with zipper T-shirts and spiked dog collars, lace doilies stitched onto T-shirts teamed with biker-style jackets and tulle cardigans. The show also included a handful of womenswear looks such as trousers that were a patchwork of lace and patterned scraps worn with a T-shirt featuring the photograph from the invitation. Both sexes sported brooches and frilly ankle socks. The overall look was a seductive mix of youthful, carefree and raw-edged that confirmed the great things expected of the designer.

Show
Spring/Summer
2011

Date/Time
22nd September 2010
11am

Place
Somerset House
The Strand
London

Format/Size
Card
20.5cm x 14.5cm
(8in x 5¾in)

Ninivah Khomo

Just a handful of guests were invited to an intimate presentation at the sumptuously decorated home of the designer Ninivah Khomo, a mix of Chinoiserie, bijoux antiques, gilded lilies and fierce animal print. With the fragrance of *Savage Vanilla* heavy in the air and champagne served in gilt-edged flutes, models that included the designer's daughter Delilah (pictured on the invitation) mingled with the guests, who sat on settees and ornamental chairs. As Khomo drew inspiration from the nostalgic looks of the 1930s the ambience was appropriately akin to a yesteryear salon show. She showed edited looks from her collection that included her signature leopard print and lace alongside sheer and opaque spiralling stripes that referenced Elsa Schiaparelli, Norman Hartnell and Chanel. There was a relaxed feeling of Deauville, as Khomo offered long striped jersey dresses-cum-rugby shirts coloured pale china blue and coffee, offset by black and white.

Show
Spring/Summer
2007

Date/Time
20th September 2006
9.45am

Place
Flat 3
30 Cadogan Place
London

Format/Size
Card
20.5cm x 14.5cm
(8in x 5¾in)

Clements Ribeiro

In the 1990s, Clements Ribeiro were the must-see show at London Fashion Week, but a decade on and beset with production problems, the husband-and-wife duo of Suzanne Clements and Ignacio Ribeiro decided to forego a costly, full-blown catwalk show and instead chose an intimate presentation in a trendy bar in London's Knightsbridge. With the pair's attention to detail channelled into just 19 outfits, they offered a collection that looked fresh and desirable when viewed up close and personal. The mood was less is more, with the naive folk art bird print on the invitation transposed onto a coat that opened the showing, and also onto other garments and bags featured throughout the line-up. This print was juxtaposed with graphic circles and the stripes that are the duo's signature. Clements Ribeiro's newest offering that season was a rugby top, which added a sporty mood to their repertoire, and a bold floral print appliquéd with rubber petals; these also featured on playful sunhats and necklaces.

Show
Spring/Summer
2006

Date/Time
19th September 2005
6.15pm

Place
Mint
164 Sloane Street
London

Format/Size
Card
15cm x 21cm
(6in x 8½in)

ROBERT CARY-WILLIAMS
SPRING / SUMMER 2006
last of england

Show
Spring/Summer
2006

Date/Time
21st September 2005
4pm

Place
British Fashion Council
Tent
Natural History Museum
Cromwell Road
London

Format/Size
Paper (unfolded)
42cm x 59cm
(16in x 23in)

Robert Cary-Williams

The designer Robert Cary-Williams has steadfastly worked outside the confines of the fashion industry, so it was not surprising to discover that the catwalk for this particular show was constructed from old doors or that the soundtrack included wartime airplanes dog-fighting overhead. The one-time marine's predilection for military style not only meant a khaki-coloured palette and fatigue-inspired silhouettes but also influenced how he utilized fabrics, which were shredded, burned and deconstructed within an inch of their lives – perhaps the aftermath of war? He also embroidered dresses with shattered glass in place of crystal. A smattering of sequins added a nod to glamour, although these were encased in the bare bones of a ballgown that was home to several starlings. Cary-Williams also added a pair of vast shoulder pads-cum-epaulettes to a draped khaki dress that featured a dragoon of tiny toy soldiers.

At the end of the show, the swarthy designer appeared with his baby son, Henry Hunter Macintosh, cradled under a heavily tattooed arm.

Todd Oldham

Texas-born Todd Oldham was always a bit of an oddball outsider on the New York fashion scene. However, his brand of colourful, zany designs soon earned him recognition (he won the Perry Ellis Award for New Fashion Talent in 1991, just two years after launching his label) and an enthusiastic fan base that included supermodels Linda Evangelista and Naomi Campbell, who loved to walk his runway. Oldham's eclectic style referenced traditional American crafts such as needlepoint and patchwork and his designs often included lavish beadwork and embroidery, as featured in the blurry image on the invitation.

For this collection, based on the work of Charles and Ray Eames, the designer offered just three prints combined with bankers' grey and navy blue. His work invariably paid homage to Alexander Girard, one of Oldham's design heroes, whom he honoured with a 672-page book dedicated to his career. Like Girard, Oldham is a multidisciplined designer and has gone on to work in graphics, architecture and product design. The invitation's flipside also featured Oldham's cartoony crown logo.

Show
Spring/Summer
1997

Date/Time
29th October 1996
7pm

Place
The Tent
Bryant Park
6th Avenue at 41st Street
New York

Format/Size
Card
22cm x 14cm
(8½in x 5½in)

Proenza Schouler

Show
Spring/Summer
2006

Date/Time
September 2005

Place
Milk Studios
450 West 15th Street
New York

Format/Size
Paper
28cm x 21.5cm
(11in x 8½in)

US *Vogue* editor Anna Wintour has described the instant success of Jack McCollough and Lazaro Hernandez, who took their mothers' maiden names for their label, as "a little fairytale". Barneys New York department store bought their final graduation collection at Parson's School of Design, on which they collaborated (a first for the art school). The pair has quickly defined their own take on modern glamour and luxury – a chic sophistication with an underlying eroticism. Proenza Schouler always begin designing their collections with fabrics and textiles, often custom made and complex. Sequins might be made of rubber or perforated leather is printed to look like tweed. The duo put their attention to detail and intricate textures down to their OCD! For this collection, which they described as "a minimal baroque", they favoured Arts and Crafts. It was "a reaction to industrialization, to mass everything," they said. This meant openwork embroidery and lace, burlap, linen, suede and velvet in shades of wheat, smoke, chartreuse, charcoal and silver.

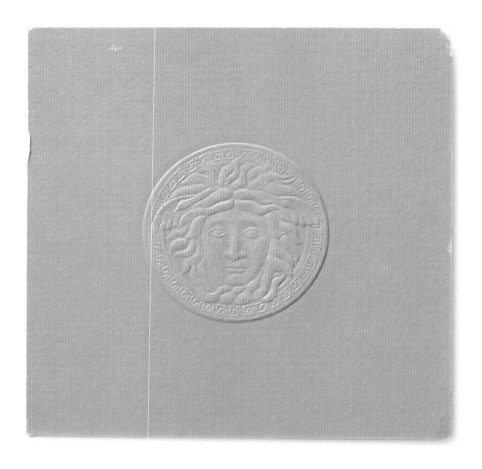

Versace

The marbled basement of the Ritz Hotel in Paris became the regular venue for Versace's atelier shows, with models parading on a catwalk that covered the hotel's swimming pool beneath. The grass green invitation hinted at the designer's eye-popping palette – verdant green was matched with strong citrus shades. Versace's daywear had a sophisticated, ladylike look harking back to the 1960s neatness of Jackie Kennedy, but cut in crazy paving optical prints and fierce animal patterns the look still had plenty of rock'n'roll attitude. As did his front row guests that included Jon Bon Jovi, Bryan Ferry and Sting, and the soundtrack featuring Elton John. Stella Tennant, who opened and closed the show, embodied the new Versace woman – strong, elegant but a touch quirky. For after-dark the designer boldly clashed leather and lace, zebra and leopard, accessorized with feathers.

Versace took his bow wearing trademark black leather, with Tennant dressed as a rock'n'roll bride in a slinky white, see-through lace gown.

Show
Haute Couture
Spring/Summer 1996

Date/Time
20th January 1996
7pm

Place
Hotel Ritz
1–2 place Vendôme
Paris

Format/Size
Card
12cm x 12cm
(4¾in x 4¾in)

A FAERIE TALE

ZANDRA RHODES   BILL GIBB   OSSIE CLARK
BELLVILLE SASSOON   BRUCE OLDFIELD
JASPER CONRAN   EMANUEL   MODERN CLASSICS

are generously loaning their Ball-Gowns and inviting you to participate in an

EVENING JOURNEY INTO THE REALMS OF FANTASY AND IMAGINATION

in aid of

THE MARIA SCLERODERMA THERAPY TRUST

regd. charity no. 274368

at

THE PARK LANE HOTEL BALLROOM

NOVEMBER 27th 1980
COCKTAILS 7.30 p.m.
TICKETS £15.00

THANKSGIVING DAY
SHOW 8.30/10.00 p.m.

A Faerie Tale

This group charity show, in aid of the Maria Scleroderma Therapy Trust, featured a selection of British fashion's best-known eveningwear designers – Zandra Rhodes, Bill Gibb, Ossie Clark, Bellville Sassoon, Bruce Oldfield and the Emanuels. It also included two names that, at the time, were relatively new to the business: Jasper Conran and Modern Classics, the hip-and-happening label designed by Willie Brown. The event was billed as "an evening journey into the realms of fantasy and imagination" and this was certainly illustrated by the portrait of model Vivienne Lynn, pictured on the invitation. Lynn was Brown's house model but also the poster-girl of the alternative Arts Set that inhabited Chelsea and Kensington and included Rhodes, jeweller Andrew Logan and artist Duggie Fields.

Such charity shows were tremendously popular as fashion designers were becoming viewed as celebrities and people were happy to pay to get a glimpse of the glamorous world they inhabited.

Show
"A Faerie Tale"
charity fashion show

Date/Time
27th November 1980
7.30pm

Place
Ballroom
The Park Lane Hotel
London

Format/Size
Card
24.5cm x 15.5cm
(9½in x 6in)

BETTY JACKSON WINTER '97

Betty Jackson

Betty Jackson's invitation and programme, featuring photo-copied images of sequins and lace, highlighted two of the main themes in the collection, while the catwalk, strewn with a drift of paper confetti leaves, defined the colour palette for the season: plum, camel, lilac, toast, grey and gold. The resulting mix was pure Jackson, a contrasting combination of the fragile and the cosy, epitomized by lace panels twisted around a chiffon petticoat-style dress, topped with a roomy ribbed sweater and shown alongside a yeti-style sheepskin robe coat. Oversized chunky-knit cardigans were worn over long lace dresses, lacy dresses over skinny pants, and a pebble-dashed tweed coat over a sequin slip dress. These juxtapositions continued throughout the show for a look the designer described as "vaguely eccentric". They were finished off with woolly scarves, sheepskin wraps, ostrich feathers and suede lace-up desert boots. Punk bird's-nest hairstyles and blush-pink make-up were the work of Kerry Warn and Carol Brown respectively.

Show
Autumn/Winter
1997–98

Date/Time
25th February 1997
12.30pm

Place
British Fashion Council Tent
Natural History Museum
Cromwell Road
London

Format/Size
Card
15cm x 21cm
(6in x 8½in)

Julien Macdonald

Having specialized in knitwear design at Brighton and the Royal College of Art, London, Macdonald's innovative cobwebby designs became an instant success. The designer made his debut at London Fashion Week in Autumn/ Winter 1997 with "Mermaids", a static presentation featuring photography by Sean Ellis, styled by Isabella Blow, who had taken the fledgling designer under her wing. Macdonald's designs were modelled by Honor Fraser, Erin O'Connor, Iris Palmer, Plum Sykes, Paula Thomas and Jodie Kidd, pictured here on the invitation. This dress was selected by Blow, then fashion director of *The Sunday Times Style* magazine, for the 1997 Dress of the Year award at the Fashion Museum in Bath. Kidd was the perfect model for Macdonald's otherworldly collection, a luminescent, mystical creature – part mermaid, part space alien. The designer is now best known for his ultra-glamorous red carpet gowns worn by Beyoncé, Kylie Minogue and Kelly Brook. He describes his designs as "sexy, high octane, powerful and liberating". His favourite word is "glamour".

Show
Autumn/Winter
1997–98

Date/Time
February 1997

Place
Imagination Gallery
25 Store Street
London

Format/Size
Card
21cm x 10cm
(8½in x 4in)

Billy Boy

Billy Boy's love of 1950s glamour and Surrealist art merged when the flamboyant club kid and self-taught designer launched Surreal Couture from his apartment in the 1970s. An avid collector of vintage fashion, especially Schiaparelli, his eccentric designs included newsprint gowns, Eiffel Tower dresses and lobster tuxedos. Lobsters also featured on this invitation. The Austrian-born, American-raised designer also created costume jewels that he described as "cartoon Chanel, as if Daisy Duck were designing her own jewellery". These became a favourite of Diana Vreeland and Andy Warhol.

Billy Boy's longtime love of dolls led to the designer giving Mattel's Barbie a makeover and creating "Le Nouveau Theatre de la Mode Barbie", with gowns by international designers. In 1989 he launched Mdvanii, a glamorous art doll with a luxurious wardrobe. Like one of Galliano's real-life mannequins, the doll was given a complex backstory by Billy Boy that involved bisexuality and Soraya, her psychic Indian friend. Mdvanii's portrait was painted by René Gruau.

Show
Haute Couture
Summer/Autumn
1982

Date/Time
15th April 1982
9pm

Place
Underground
860 Broadway
New York

Format/Size
Card
18cm x 12.5cm
(7in x 5in)

Show
Menswear
Autumn/Winter
2010–11

Date/Time
18th January 2010
7pm

Place
Spazio Revel
Via Thaon de Revel, 3
Milan

Format/Size
Card
21cm x 15cm
(8¼in x 6in)

Alexander McQueen

The floor, walls and columns of the art gallery location were covered in a digital mosaic-like design that integrated Alexander McQueen's signature skull design into the pattern. This backdrop, somewhere between tribal decoration and Byzantine fresco, informed the collection from the soft blush, brown and grey palette to the layered prints. The musician Sting, who appeared on the invitation in a photograph by David Burton, also performed on the soundtrack, singing songs from his 2009 album, *If On A Winter's Night*, featuring traditional English songs dating back to the fourteenth century.

McQueen's models had a deathly pallor and severe bowl-cut hairdos that gave them the look of medieval monasticism. Some wore menacing balaclavas or half-masks as they paraded solemnly through the space in sleekly tailored ensembles that were rich in pattern – from Pagan corn plaits to a ghostly skeletal design. The skull appeared again, knitted into a chunky sweater edged with fur. Tragically, less than a month after this show, the designer committed suicide.

Dolce & Gabbana

Domenico Dolce and Stefano Gabbana hosted a party for Kylie Minogue to celebrate the singer's "KylieFever2002" tour, for which they had exclusively designed the costumes. Held in a vast warehouse in Milan, the ambience was part-discotheque, part-Bacchanalian feast. The event featured handsome male models, cast as Roman centurions, in attendance on invited guests including the international fashion press, who spent the evening lounging on banquettes coiffing champagne. Costumes for the tour included a futuristic silver ensemble, urban combat pants, a long black evening gown and the pink-and-black basque Ms Minogue wore during her performance of "In Your Eyes", which referenced Dolce & Gabbana's love of corsetry. The duo worked with the singer again for her "Showgirl" and "Aphrodite" tours.

Kylie Minogue's list of costume designers reads like a Who's Who of fashion and includes Jean Paul Gaultier, John Galliano, Stephen Jones, Fee Doran for Mrs Jones, Julien Macdonald, Gareth Pugh, Christopher Kane and Stevie Stewart.

Show
Kylie Minogue party

Date/Time
18th June 2002
Late

Place
Via Malipiero
Milan

Format/Size
Card
7cm x 10.5cm
(2¾in x 4in)

John Galliano

For this collection, entitled "Forgotten Innocents", a baby-faced Helena Bonham Carter, flush from the critical success of *Room With A View*, appeared on the invitation. The show started with Sibylle de Saint Phalle, who worked with Galliano, playing with a child's cat's cradle made out of wool. This set the mood for a collection that Galliano described as akin to children playing dress-up. Yet this show marked a distinct maturing that saw the designer focusing his twisted seams and experimental cutting. Exquisitely tailored pale blue and creamy white ensembles evoked a peculiar purity. Models wore coronets created by Judy Blame, who fashioned them from playing cards and bits of scrap metal scavenged from the banks of the River Thames. Another club kid, Patrick Cox, made the shoes while William A Casey did the make-up and Ray Allington added ankle-length Rapunzel-style braids. At this time Galliano was making a bid to secure his business with backing by Danish entrepreneur Peder Bertelsen of Aguecheek.

Show
Autumn/Winter
1986–87

Date/Time
March 1986

Place
Duke of York Barracks
King's Road
London

Format/Size
Card
38cm x 16cm
(15in x 6¼in)

Frost French

Sadie Frost and Jemima French eschewed the traditional catwalk show in favour of something closer to Ms Frost's entertainment roots, a mini-performance entitled "Girl". The stage, decorated with giant blow-ups of the illustrations (by Tasha) that featured in the programme, showcased girlish vignettes by the designers' celebrity friends. This show was all about the casting: "cool girl" Kate Moss, "soul girl" Leah Wood, "rock chick girl" Rosemary Ferguson and as narrator, actress Lisa Faulkner. Each girl acted her way through a somewhat lightweight narrative while "dressing and undressing" in and out of the clothes on show – mostly a selection of pretty vintage-style dresses, urban denim and the sexy satin underwear that the designers were famous for. The mood was all very girly and a little bit saucy, the kind of pose a teenage girl might strike when pretending to be burlesque dancer Dita Von Teese. Frost French favoured oddball presentations – another show was staged at the Open Air Theatre in Regent's Park, London.

Show
Autumn/Winter
2002–3

Date/Time
17th February 2002
5.30pm

Place
The Duke of York's Theatre
St Martin's Lane
London

Format/Size
Booklet
25cm x 17.5cm
(9¾in x 7in)

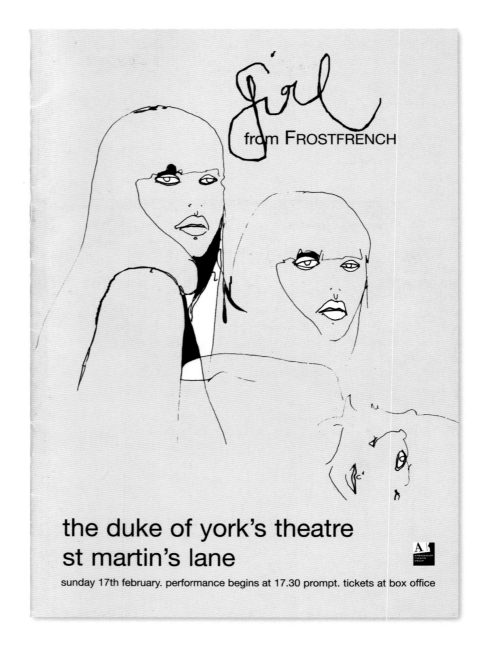

the duke of york's theatre
st martin's lane

sunday 17th february. performance begins at 17.30 prompt. tickets at box office

Cerruti

Cerruti design director Narciso Rodriguez achieved worldwide acclaim when he was chosen by Carolyn Bessette to design her wedding dress for her marriage to John F. Kennedy Jr. in 1996. He described the starting point for this particular collection as "a single flower", specifically a bougainvillea in an amazing shade of black-red. This coloured his collection, starting with the striking red invitation featuring a graphic portrait of Kate Moss that offers an image that veers toward Hitchcockian drama to the matte red lipstick worn by the models in the show. Moss also starred in the label's advertising campaign, photographed by Paolo Roversi.

In this collection the designer played with contrasts throughout, explaining that he wanted to emphasize the strength of the jacket and the sensuality of the dress. In the 1960s Nino Cerruti, one of fashion's most stylish men, aimed to blur the sexes on the runways, creating an androgynous look that was modern in spirit but embedded in the heritage and tradition of men's tailoring.

Show
Autumn/Winter
1997–98

Date/Time
March 1997

Place
Paris

Format/Size
Card
29cm x 18cm
(11½in x 7in)

Geoffrey Beene

Geoffrey Beene was a design pioneer who worked outside the industry. He showed his designs off-schedule in his showroom or explored different ways of presenting them in staged productions that involved film or dance. This 32-minute film, called "30", made in collaboration with director Tom Kalin, was commissioned to mark three decades in the fashion industry. Shot in black-and-white, it lovingly evoked the silent film era and features an ensemble cast, including a young Claire Danes. The independent filmmaker has also directed *Swoon* (1992). This short film offered a sensual narrative that was a celebration of Beene's timeless creativity and his languid and sometimes stark designs. There was also a magazine created especially for the occasion.

Beene was the ultimate modernist, making ballgowns of grey flannel and jersey and creating iconic American football shirts stitched in sequins. The first American designer to show in Milan and the winner of eight Coty awards since launching his label in 1963, Beene died in 2004.

Show
Spring/Summer
1994

Date/Time
3rd November 1993
7pm

Place
The Theatre
The Equitable
787 Seventh Avenue
New York

Format/Size
Card
25.5cm x 18cm
(10in x 7in)

"A really well made Buttonhole is the only link between Art and Nature."
Oscar Wilde

ROCHAS

prie

Monsieur Jan R. Webb

de lui faire l'honneur d'assister au dîner de présentation de

la Collection Automne-Hiver 1997–1998

le Dimanche 16 Mars 1997 à 21 heures.

Villa Barclay
3, avenue Matignon
75008 Paris

Salon : **A**

R.S.V.P : carton-réponse ci-joint
Bureau de presse :
Béatrice Keller - Tél. 01 45 44 50 65

Invitation strictement personnelle

Parking rond-point des Champs-Elysées
Entrée face au 1, avenue Matignon

Show
Autumn/Winter
1997–98

Date/Time
16th March 1997
9pm

Place
Villa Barclay
3 Avenue Matignon
Paris

Format/Size
Card
21cm x 30cm
(8¼in x 11¾in)

Rochas

Designer Peter O'Brien's couture aesthetic and love of old-school Hollywood glamour (his final St Martin's School of Art collection included silver and lavender taffeta and organza gowns) earned him the top role as designer-in-chief at the French fashion house Rochas. For this supper show, guests sat at tables heavy with silverware, crystal, floral arrangements and twinkling candles. The invitation and programme featured quotes from fellow Irishman Oscar Wilde, Dorothy Parker and George Bernard Shaw, alongside illustrations by O'Brien. Outfits were named after actresses: a chocolate "first night" dress was called Kay Kendall, a blue chiffon dress was Bea Arthur, and a silk panne velvet ensemble was named after Margo Channing/Eve Harrington. The soundtrack mirrored the programme's Broadway namedropping, mixing Stephen Sondheim with a song called "Marriage Is For Single Girls" from Burt Bacharach's 1968 musical, *Promises, Promises*, and Elaine Stritch singing "Are You Having Any Fun?" The finale featured "Night Waltz" from *A Little Night Music*.

John Galliano

When editors received this clutch bag containing a deep purple lipstick, streamers, used matchbook and an unidentified pill, it offered a clue to the outrageous antics to follow. The bag also contained crumpled bank notes, bearing a portrait of John Galliano sporting a top hat and 'tache, that later fell from the ceiling during the show's finale. On arrival at the venue, a cabaret club on the outskirts of Paris, guests were greeted by women proffering suffragette-style manifesto leaflets advocating Female Fashion Reform. The soundtrack confirmed the mood as Liza Minnelli and Joel Grey performed a funked-up version of "Money" from the movie *Cabaret*. Under twinkling lights the models posed among exotic extras dressed as habitués of the demi-monde, their faces caked with make-up, sporting top hats, feather boas and stockings and suspenders – and that was just the men! Galliano's twilight world melded the Berlin of William S. Burroughs and Luchino Visconti's 1969 film, *The Damned*. Models, including Linda Evangelista, Eva Herzigova and Susie Bick, looked equally outré in glittering gowns and sweeping robe coats.

Show
Autumn/Winter
1998–99

Date/Time
March 1998

Place
Cabaret Sauvage
parc de la Viollette
211 avenue Jean Jaurès
Paris

Format/Size
Purse, assorted contents
13cm x ?17cm
(5¼in x 7in)

Antoni & Alison

To mark their twentieth anniversary design duo Antoni Burakowski and Alison Roberts invited the London Fashion Week audience to "the premiere of 'The Party Portraits'". The showing of this 15-minute film was made all the more exciting as it was rumoured to star Hollywood A-lister Nicole Kidman, a longtime friend of the designers. However, Antoni & Alison are not the type to flaunt their celebrity friendships and so the film was screened only once. The accompanying lookbook meanwhile was censored with Ms Kidman's famous features hidden by a black anonymity strip (the type used in sex scandals) and the actress was only identifiable by her famous flame-red hair. The designers cast Ms Kidman in a variety of roles from "a woman who hates her skirt" to "a woman in the wrong dress for a party", as she modelled 21 of the duo's pretty designs, along with a selection of party hats and balloons. Cinemagoers were given iced birthday cakes.

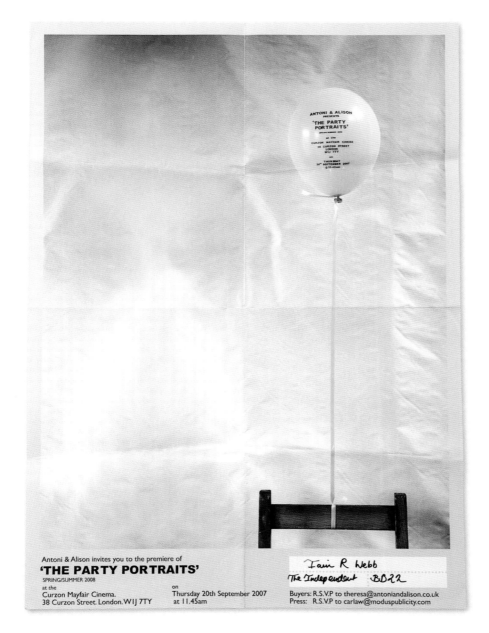

Antoni & Alison invites you to the premiere of
'THE PARTY PORTRAITS'
SPRING/SUMMER 2008

at the
Curzon Mayfair Cinema.
38 Curzon Street. London. W1J 7TY

on
Thursday 20th September 2007
at 11.45am

Iain R Webb
The Independent BD22

Buyers: R.S.V.P to theresa@antoniandalison.co.uk
Press: R.S.V.P to carlaw@moduspublicity.com

Show
Spring/Summer
2008

Date/Time
20th September 2007
11.45am

Place
Curzon Mayfair Cinema
38 Curzon Street
London

Format/Size
Poster
42cm x 59.5cm
(16½in x 23½in)
Booklet
21cm x 15cm
(8½in x 6in)

Raf Simons

Having originally studied Industrial and Furniture Design, Belgian Raf Simons made the leap to menswear in 1995. Best known for his pursuit of modernity and innovation, at this ultra-minimal presentation Simons continued to challenge convention by reworking standard-looking suits with a cut-up of panel pieces that mimicked the invitation. During the show, these suits morphed into urban protective wear, while sweaters were elongated to become knee-length dresses worn over cigarette-thin trousers. Simons also explored a dramatically new silhouette that featured a padded corset and bell-shaped, button-through skirt, again worn over trousers. The same outline defined defiantly un-classic trench coats. This new proposition appeared to reference Christian Dior's equally shocking New Look "Carolle" or "Figure 8" silhouette of 1947. With hindsight these explorations seem prescient, given that two years later Simons would assume the role of creative director at the House of Dior. Then again, he is a designer who has always displayed a remarkable insight into the future.

Show
Menswear
Autumn/Winter
2010–11

Date/Time
23rd January 2010
9pm

Place
Jeu de Paume
1 place de la Concorde
Paris

Format/Size
Card, sticker
14.5cm x 21cm
(5¾in x 8¼in)

Show
Haute Couture
Autumn/Winter
2001–2

Date/Time
7th July 2001
2pm

Place
École Nationale
Supérieure des Beaux-Arts
14 rue Bonaparte
Paris

Format/Size
Plastic badge, card
3cm x 3cm
(1in x 1in)

Christian Dior

At this time creative director John Galliano had begun to deconstruct the monolithic label and was keen to introduce modern-day iconography. Collections featured trashy beauty queens and footballing heroes mixed up with religious imagery and referenced popular musical genres such as punk and hip-hop. For the Dior Autumn/Winter 2001 show the models resembled ravers en route to Goa via a field off the M25. Wielding ghetto-blaster bags on their shoulders and layered with colour and pattern, they sported pull-on woolly hats and T-shirts decorated with the CD logo reconfigured as the blissed-out Smiley Face. Galliano continued the theme in his Dior Haute Couture Autumn/Winter 2001 collection.

To the live accompaniment of the orchestra of the National Opera of Paris, South Sudanese model Alek Wek emerged, wearing a multicoloured tie-dye chiffon gown emblazoned with the smiley logo and marijuana leaves. When challenged about these motifs of drug use in an interview for *V* magazine, Galliano responded: "They're part of popular culture."

Anna Sui

The invitation pictures Anna Sui's unique boutique at 113 Greene Street in the trendy Soho district of New York. The illustration by Dean "Chooch" Landry replicates the soot-black shop front with its engraved stained-glass windows featuring Sui's trademark dolly head. The Art Nouveau black and purple colour palette is core to the designer's brand and has also been used for her fragrance, jewellery and packaging, as well as the stores' interior. This colour combination also appeared in this collection, which was inspired by the Ballets Russes exhibition at the Victoria & Albert Museum in London, from the catwalk and backdrop that mimicked the boutique's interior to the richly patterned clothes. As ever, Sui's designs were a mix of romantic and rock'n'roll, Mod meets Dandy, referencing the Ormsby-Gore sisters who were the trendsetters of London in the Swinging Sixties, when they took to wearing the original Ballets Russes costumes designed by Leon Bakst. Sui took her bows wearing a purple floral dress.

Show
Autumn/Winter
2011–12

Date/Time
16th February 2011
6pm

Place
Lincoln Center
The Theatre
Columbus Avenue at 63rd Street
New York

Format/Size
Card
17.8cm x 12.7cm
(7in x 5in)

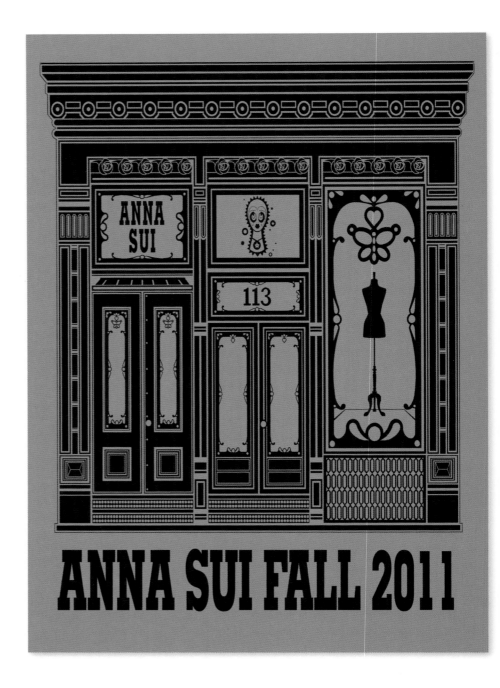

Marni

Date/Time
5th October 2003
9am

Place
Sala Ventunoprimo
Largo Domodossola, 1
Milan

Format/Size
Card
13½cm x 27cm
(5¾in x 11in)

The Marni show always means an early start so designer Consuelo Castiglioni kindly provides a shot of strong coffee to perk up the sleepy audience on its way into the draughty, white-washed warehouse space. Yet, inevitably it is Castiglioni's collection that lifts the front row's spirits with a playful mix of colour and pattern. Castiglioni is a designer who relishes the sheer enjoyment of clothes and this season was no different. At the heart of the Marni look is a naive wonderment, almost a little dressmaker in feel, and this season Castiglioni picked up on the 1950s mood that permeated elsewhere on the catwalks. Of course none of this would have been hinted at by the utilitarian invitation – although perhaps the favoured shade of tomato meets salmon (the same shade as the coat worn by model Elise Crombez to open the show) was a hint at the off-kilter, summery palette – dusty pink, sherbert lemon, washed-out watery blues and faded mint and chocolate brown. Uplifting and joyous throughout.

Mugler

Italian/Japanese Nicola Formichetti is one of the fashion industry's most respected editors/art directors; he was also the stylist of groundbreaking pop phenomenon Lady Gaga. In 2010, Formichetti was named creative director of the mens- and womenswear lines at Thierry Mugler, the French fashion house that was rebranding itself, following the exit of the eponymous designer. The label was simply renamed Mugler, with Formichetti reinforcing this strategic change by repeating the same invitation design across several seasons.

   The new-look Mugler, encapsulated by the functional, futuristic-style logo, followed in the footsteps of the brand's namesake, who specialized in a fashion-forward sci-fi look. He would no doubt have approved of the appearance on the catwalk of Lady Gaga and Rick Genest (aka "Zombie Boy"), a male model tattooed to resemble a skeleton. Gaga also provided the soundtrack. Formichetti has since left the brand with Thierry Mugler returning as "creative advisor".

Show
Menswear
Autumn/Winter 2011–12
Autumn/Winter 2012–13
Spring/Summer 2013

Date/Time
19th January 2011, 6pm
18th January 2012, 6pm
27th June 2012, 6.30pm

Place
Paris

Format/Size
Card
15cm x 20cm
(6in x 7¾in)

Show
Spring/Summer 1976
Spring/Summer 2007

Date/Time
October 1975
20th September 2006

Place
The Roundhouse, Chalk
Farm, London
The British Fashion
Council Tent, Natural
History Museum,
Cromwell Road,
London

Format/Size
Card
28.5cm x 22.5cm
(11¼in x 9in)

Zandra Rhodes

For the presentation of her 1976 collection, inspired by a trip across America in a Volkswagen campervan, Zandra Rhodes chose the Roundhouse, at the time a cutting-edge arts venue that suited her radical style. The staging included giant cutout cacti, as featured on the fan invitation (stuffed satin versions featured in her West End shop), around which the models danced. Her chiffon designs were printed with cacti and arrowheads, while Ultrasuede was cut into gaucho skirts and chaps. These were accessorized with bejewelled ZR 'kerchiefs and authentic cowboy boots purchased during her trip. A young fashion student called Ben Scholten appeared as a cowboy in the show; he would later become Rhodes' design director. The soundtrack included Ferde Grofé and Jerry Jeff Walker.

Rhodes' 2007 collection reworked many of her greatest hits (including the fan) – colourful swirling prints, wafting kaftans, puffball skirts and lettuce-edged metallic eveningwear. This show was styled by Karen Binns and included glittering jewellery by Andrew Logan and hats by Stephen Jones.

Paul Smith

My Wardrobe Nicola Copping

PAUL SMITH HAS THE PLEASURE OF INVITING

TO HIS AUTUMN WINTER 2013 SHOW
ON SUNDAY 17TH FEBRUARY 2013 AT 7PM

TATE BRITAIN
THE MANTON ENTRANCE
ATTERBURY STREET
LONDON SW1P4RG

PRESS ENQUIRIES: ZOE MEADS
LFWPRESSTICKETS@PAULSMITH.CO.UK
020 7257 6664

SALES ENQUIRIES: STUART HOWIE
LFWBUYERTICKETS@PAULSMITH.CO.UK
020 7836 7828

BC27

Paul Smith

Paul Smith likes to wave the flag for Britain, staging his fashion shows in diverse venues, from the luxury of Claridges to outdoor locations such as the Orangery in Holland Park or a gritty urban underpass in darkest Bermondsey. This season Smith chose the imposing industrial architecture of the Tate Britain's East Wing as a monochromatic modernist backdrop for his colourful collection. This was not the only contrast: eye-popping hues clashed with navy, rust, off-white and a glint of silver, while fabrics ranged from cosy alpaca and felted wool to shimmering layered organza. Smith offered a post-punk, new wave silhouette – think slouch-shouldered jackets and knife-sharp trousers. This look was emphasized with a soundtrack devised by Peter Smith and Andrew Hale, who put together a playlist of electronica (old and new) to suggest what they described as a "pop-up art school disco". Smith's use of a formal style invitation printed on a sheet of electric blue Perspex was the perfect scene-setter.

Show
Autumn/Winter
2013–14

Time/Date
17th February 2013
7pm

Place
Tate Britain
Atterbury Street
London

Format/Size
Perspex
10.5cm x14.8cm
(4⅛ in x 5⅞ in)

Show
Autumn/Winter
2013–14

Date/Time
16th February 2013
12pm

Place
Somerset House
The Strand
London

Format/Size
Perspex
14.5cm x 21cm
(5¾in x 8in)

Jasper Conran

Guests receiving Jasper Conran's fluorescent Perspex invitation were right to assume that bright colour would feature in his show, however nothing could have prepared them for the blistering display on the catwalk, itself fashioned from vivid orange lacquered panels. This hi-gloss theme continued throughout the collection, with cute patent pumps and a series of sparkling sequin dresses in blood orange, shocking pink and pillar-box red.

Asked why he went crazy for colour in a winter collection, the designer said it was his attempt to cheer people up during such miserable times. And that certainly was the effect of the bold Pop-Art hues. Conran's other key style reference was the Swinging Sixties, a period of optimism. He reworked simple A-line shift dresses, pleated miniskirts and neat coats, as worn by actress Mia Farrow, in satin, wool, leather and fur. This upbeat collection was accessorized with matching opaque tights and flowerpot felt hats by milliner Stephen Jones.

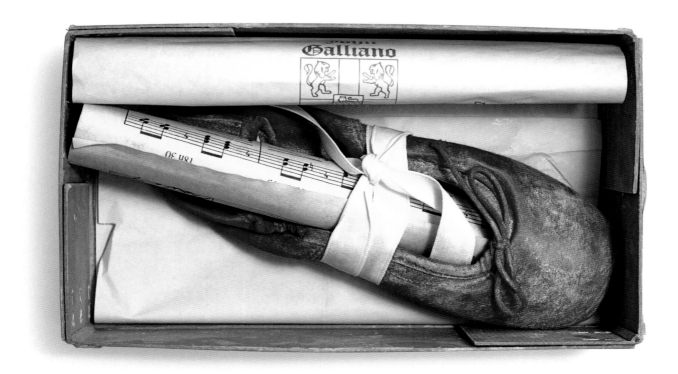

John Galliano

Another masterpiece theatrical production, appropriately staged in the Parisian playhouse where the celebrated Russian ballet dancer Nijinsky had performed the scandalous Rite of Spring in 1913. The sheet music was part of an elaborate box of tricks also containing a ballet pointe shoe. As crowds fought to get inside the theatre, guests took their seats, including a number positioned onstage. Galliano had said he wanted them to experience the crazy backstage ambience and smell the greasepaint so models gave a tour de force performance as they emerged through trap doors and wandered the aisles, acting out the designer's latest fantasy.

The loose narrative for this collection included a female version of William Golding's novel, *Lord of the Flies*, Boldini's "Contessa Casati" (a constant inspiration for Galliano), Degas' ballerinas (model Shalom Harlow wearing a frou-frou tutu pirouetted bravely on the balcony!) and Romanian sculptor Brancusi. In clothes terms that translated as a mix of embroidered broderie anglaise ruffles, bias-cut satin and taffeta evening gowns and sleek grey and black suiting.

Show
Spring/Summer
1996

Date/Time
15th October 1995
6.30pm

Place
Théâtre des Champs Elysées
15 avenue Montaigne
Paris

Format/Size
Cardboard box, fabric, paper
12cm x 21cm x 6cm
(4¾in x 8¼in x 2½in)

Valentino

When the front row arrived to take their seats at a Valentino show in the early 1990s, they found a cassette tape on every seat featuring the soundtrack to the collection. This compilation segued quite diverse artists and tracks, including Dan Hartman's "Name of the Game", A-ha's "Take on Me", Propaganda's "Duel" and "Dancin'" by Chris Isaak, along with the atmospheric sound of a telephone ringing off the hook. Valentino's shows were classy affairs, with a continual ebbing and flowing of supermodels such as Yasmeen Ghauri, Marpessa Hennink and Karen Mulder, who boasted big sunglasses, big jewels, and even bigger hair. The traditional finale to a Valentino show saw the designer saunter down the catwalk, one hand casually in a pocket, the other outstretched, waving to his faithful fan club of swanky society ladies in the front row. To accompany this parade, "New York, New York" by Frank Sinatra.

Show
circa 1990

Place
Paris

Format/Size
Cassette tape
6.5cm x 10.5cm
(2½in x 4in)

Show
Spring/Summer 1979

Date/Time
26th September 1978
8.30pm

Place
The Embassy Club
7 Old Bond Street
London

Format/Size
Card
18.5cm x 18.5cm
(7¼in x 7¼in)

Joseph

Moroccan-born Joseph Ettedgui was an exceptional retailer in that he was one of the first to identify the shopping experience as entertainment (hence the record shaped invitation designed by Tim Lamb). In the 1970s and 1980s he masterminded an entire world of Joseph, allowing his customers to not only buy new clothes from his stores (including his eponymous label), they could also dine in his Joe's Café restaurant and adorn their homes with appropriately chic furnishings and fittings from Joseph Pour la Maison. Ettedgui understood that it was important to offer a smorgasbord of brands, so alongside wardrobe classics, he championed new names including Margaret Howell and Kenzo Takada.

For this show, staged at The Embassy Club, at the time a favourite haunt of Ettedgui's fashion pack friends, he added Claude Montana to the line-up. Norman Foster designed Ettedgui's high-tech, matt black and chrome flagship store in Sloane Street in 1979, which became the template for the Joseph brand.

Etro

Established as a textile company in 1968 by Gerolamo Etro, the label is known for its use of lush layers of pattern and print, texture and embellishment, with an ethnic feeling inspired by traditional Indian paisley designs. The overriding mood on the Etro catwalk is joyful and optimistic, which sometimes sees it out of step with the fashion industry's po-faced proclivity for cynicism and irony. For this season the advertising campaign featured a goldfish alongside model Laura Ponte, who was wearing a printed safari suit styled with desert-hued scarves. The slogan read: "La Nature des Choses?" This natural mood was continued with the use of raffia that held together the various parts of the invitation, mimicking pattern pieces. The same year Veronica Etro graduated from Central Saint Martins in London and joined the family business (she later took over as womenswear designer). The most-played song on the Milan catwalks that season was the mysterious-sounding "Cotton Wool" by the Manchester electronic trip-hop duo, Lamb.

Show
Spring/Summer
1997

Date/Time
4th October 1996
7.30pm

Place
Via Spartaco, 3
Milan

Format/Size
Card, paper, raffia
14cm x 10.5cm (largest card)
5½in x 4in)

Date/Time
22nd September 2010
3.15pm

Place
Somerset House
The Strand
London

Format/Size
Card
14.5cm x 21cm
(5¾in x 8¼in)

Carolyn Massey

Carolyn Massey, who graduated from London's Royal College of Art in 2005, launched her label the following year. She was one of 10 designers who were supported by the NewGen MEN initiative sponsored by Topman. Recipients received business support, funding and the opportunity to present their collection during London Fashion Week's menswear event.

This season Massey staged an informal presentation in the Portico Rooms at Somerset House, with guests treated to a complementary gin and tonic as they viewed the collection. The look was youthful and carefree but while Massey stated she was inspired by two books, *(un)FASHION* by Tibor Kalman and *Farm* by Jackie Nickerson, there was also a touch of Tom Sawyer in the styling, with skinny trousers rolled to the knee and straw hats perched on the back of models' heads. Massey's collection merged urban sportswear with African dress. She represents a new generation of designer who use the heritage and formality of Englishness to push the boundaries of menswear.

Jean Paul Gaultier

The order form used for Jean Paul Gaultier's invitation is the exact same type presented to buyers to enable them to purchase from his collection. This concept defined Gaultier's menswear presentation, which was staged in his expansive showroom. Instead of a catwalk and regular rows of chairs the venue was laid out as if for buying appointments, with tables and chairs scattered throughout, alongside racks of clothes. Models were corralled inside a double-height scaffolding structure and throughout the show were dressed and undressed by a team of assistants in full view of the audience. Gaultier himself was visible throughout the show.

The collection included Hawaiian prints and plaids, sheer blouson jackets and trench coats, reworked leather motorcycle jackets, and tuxedos worn with Bermuda shorts. Each of the 26 looks was photographed against a makeshift studio backdrop at one end of the showroom. For his finale parade Gaultier offered variations on his trademark Breton stripes.

Show
Menswear
Spring/Summer
2012

Date/Time
23rd June 2011
5pm

Place
325 rue Saint Martin
Paris

Format/Size
Paper purchase order
21cm x 29.5cm
(8¼in x 11½in)

Chloé

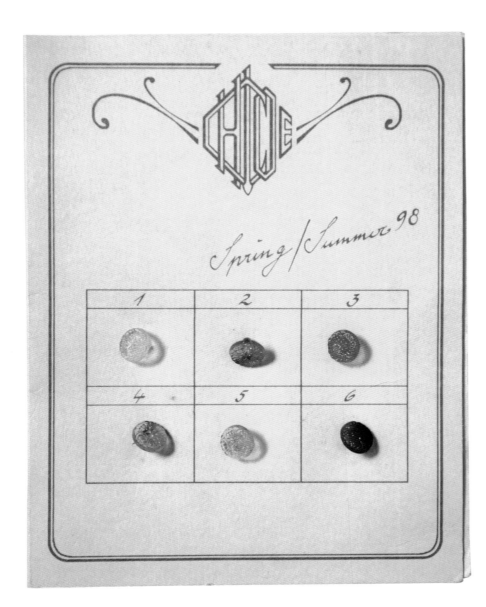

In 1997 Stella McCartney was appointed creative director at Chloé, just two years after graduating from Central Saint Martins College of Art & Design in London. The presentation of her debut collection sent the fashion pack into a frenzy. The staging of the show at the grand Parisian opera house only added to the drama, although McCartney cleverly focused her designs on the feminine heritage of the fashion house, from the delicate coloured glass buttons on the antique-look invitation card to the satin corsets and trailing taffetas that she teamed with her trademark Savile Row-style tailoring. The show provided an emotional moment, not just for the flag-waving British editors but also for McCartney's friends and family: models Kate Moss and Naomi Campbell walked her runway (as they had done for her graduation show), while Dad Paul and Mum Linda leapt from their seats to applaud their daughter's triumphant debut, alongside other music business headliners Neil Tennant and Mick Hucknall.

Show
Spring/Summer
1998

Date/Time
15 October 1997
10.30am

Place
L'Opéra Garnier
Place de l'Opéra
Paris

Format/Size
Card, buttons
17cm x 13.5cm
(6¾in x 5¼in)

Moschino

Titled "Sewing Along with Moschino",
this collection had a nostalgic "Holly
Homemaker" feel. On the catwalk
dresses were made from crochet
lace, tablecloth check, folksy tapestry
and fabrics that looked like curtains.
And, of course, there were a few
stylish jokes including Karen Elson
toting a milk-carton shoulder bag
and Erin O'Connor wearing a suit
that appeared to be scorched around
the edges (as if she had perhaps
stood too close to the stove). There
were also various reworkings of the
trench coat. How thoughtful, then,
of the fashion house to provide a
real trench coat pattern on each
seat – or was this part of Moschino's
ongoing commentary on fashion?
While inviting press and buyers to
see the label's latest retail offer, there
was also the chance for the budding
home dressmaker to fashion their own
Moschino classic. This also reinforced
how the designer always delighted in
taking wardrobe classics and giving
them his own twist.

Show
Spring/Summer
1999

Date/Time
October 1998

Place
Milan

Format/Size
Sewing pattern
27.5cm x 19.5cm
(10¾in x 7¾in)

Show
Menswear
Spring/Summer
1989

Date/Time
26th August 1988
11am

Place
49–50 Great
Marlborough Street
London

Format/Size
Card
18.5cm x 14.5cm
(7¼in x 5¾in)

Jasper Conran

Throughout his career designer Jasper Conran has used a variety of locations to present his collections, from airy art galleries and anonymous purpose-built tents to the intimacy of his West End showroom. He chose the latter for this menswear collection. Such a relaxed approach ensured that guests could experience the workmanship and subtle detailing of his designs at close range. As inferred by the image on the invitation, an old photograph used as inspiration by the designer, the collection focused on sartorial elegance. The look celebrated British tailoring with modern, stripped-down suits and waistcoats featuring quirky touches echoing his chic womenswear line. At this time navy gabardine was a favourite fabric.

Conran has always been keen to use charismatic models in his shows and was especially fond of the Kamen brothers, Nick and Barry, who appeared side-by-side several times on his catwalk. Nick's then girlfriend Talisa Soto also modelled for Conran, as did Naomi Campbell and Veronica Webb.

John Galliano

This was the first of Galliano's lavishly produced shows when the designer created his own mise en scène. A 1950s world of corsets and Cadillacs – literally, scattered around the photographic studio were several shiny American automobiles and pompadoured greasemonkeys for the models to flirt with. Galliano mixed Americana with the elegance of 1950s couture and the exoticism of Japan. Each outfit drew whoops of delight as the models preened and posed, checking their make-up in a car mirror. The end of the show signalled when a platinum blonde Linda Evangelista emerged in a vast meringue of canary yellow tulle. Uppermost in Galliano's shows is the compelling narrative. It is the stuff of fashion legend that he gave each model a detailed backstory before she would step out of the dressing room. The boxing poster and the antique book sent to guests offered a world of romance – the battered hero and the bookish heroine. A flower, perhaps a love token passed between the couple, was also included.

Show
Spring/Summer
1995

Date/Time
12th October 1994
8pm

Place
Studio Pin-Up
23 avenue Jean Moulin
Paris

Format/Size
Poster
28cm x 38cm
(11in x 15in)

Jean Paul Gaultier

The poster invitation, featuring boxing images including Sylvester Stallone as Rocky and Robert De Niro in *Raging Bull*, billed this show as "The Greatest Bout Of All Time". Jean Paul Gaultier was certainly on champion form as he juxtaposed sharp tailoring and funky sportswear. For this presentation the designer's HQ featured a ring set up for a bout by female kickboxers, modelling Gaultier's trademark tattoo tops and leather corsetry. An assortment of bruised and battered male models appeared, with hands wrapped in bandages or sporting Everlast boxing gloves. Hooded jersey tops, satin shorts and leggings were worn throughout. One worse-for-wear dandy in top hat and tails forsook his silk opera scarf for a fluffy towel.

In the 1980s Gaultier had worked with dancer Régine Chopinot to costume her ballet, *KOK*, which was also staged in a boxing ring. For this show Gaultier took his bows to Rocky's theme, wearing a towelling robe and suitably made up with a blackened eye and bloodied nose.

Show
Menswear
Autumn/Winter
2010–11

Date/Time
21st January 2010
5pm

Place
325 rue Saint-Martin
Paris

Format/Size
Poster
42cm x 29cm
(16½in x 11½in)

Central Saint Martins

In the summer of 2011 the downbeat, sprawling building in Soho that had housed St Martin's School of Art (now Central Saint Martins) since 1939 closed its doors for good as the institution moved to a new vast campus in King's Cross. The world-renowned London art school has produced a dazzling roll call of innovative and influential fashion designers, including Bill Gibb, Katharine Hamnett, Rifat Ozbek, John Galliano, Hussein Chalayan, Alexander McQueen (and Sarah Burton), Gareth Pugh and Christopher Kane.

To commemorate the event, super-stylist Katie Grand hosted a party for a few hundred of her fellow ex-fashion students to say hello and wave goodbye. The "Farewell" bash hosted past generations of graduates, from Giles Deacon to Sex Pistol Glen Matlock, who along with the original Pistols line-up played their first gig at St Martin's in 1975. On the night another former student Jarvis Cocker and his band Pulp performed a surprise final gig at the venue.

Show
"Farewell to Fashion"

Date/Time
1st June 2011
7pm

Place
St Martins School of Art
Charing Cross Road
London

Format/Size
Plastic wristband
19cm x 2cm
(7½in x ¾in)

Louis Vuitton

In 1997 the French conglomerate LVMH announced the surprise appointment of Marc Jacobs as creative director of Louis Vuitton. Even more surprising was Jacobs' debut Autumn/Winter 1998 collection for the brand, which offered a stripped-down, minimal look in white, black and grey, with touches of olive green, claret and sky blue. The collection was devoid of logos, save for the understated LV initials embossed into one leather messenger bag toted by Kirsten Owen. Yet Jacobs' remarkable vision had an immediate effect with the poster boy of New York's avant-garde transforming the somewhat tarnished bourgeois brand into one of the most coveted labels on Planet Fashion.

This LV stamped logo featured the following season on pastel-coloured backpacks, purses and even a case for a cigarette lighter. It was later used for a collection of city bags and small leather goods, called "Monogram Mat", launched in July 2002. The wristband that was part of the press kit became a cult accessory.

Show
Promotional gift

Date
July 2002

Place
Paris

Format/Size
Leather studded wristband
23cm x 4cm
(9in x 1½in)

Margaret Howell

This was one of the rare occasions when Margaret Howell showed her collection away from the security of her store. The flat lace-up man's shoe featured on the invitation has become a constant for Howell, who began her career designing men's shirts. Her aesthetic is grounded in functional, non-fussy pieces that take their inspiration from the way in which a man dresses. However, this season, perhaps while in the mood for a little experimentation (a new venue, why not a new look?), the designer was persuaded by her stylist to add a classic Nike trainer as a footwear option. However, the look of the clothes remained pure Howell, with this season's silhouette veering on frumpy. The mood was a woman in a man's world, specifically 1940s wartime – think land girls – with outfits taking inspiration from battledress jackets, men's tweedy suits (worn by pretty, scrubbed- faced girls) and trench coats. Howell made the look fresh with pastels and floral prints.

Show
Spring/Summer
1997

Date/Time
26th September 1996
4pm

Place
West Lawn Tent
Natural History Museum
Cromwell Road
London

Format/Size
Card
22.5cm x 17.5cm
(8¾in x 7in)

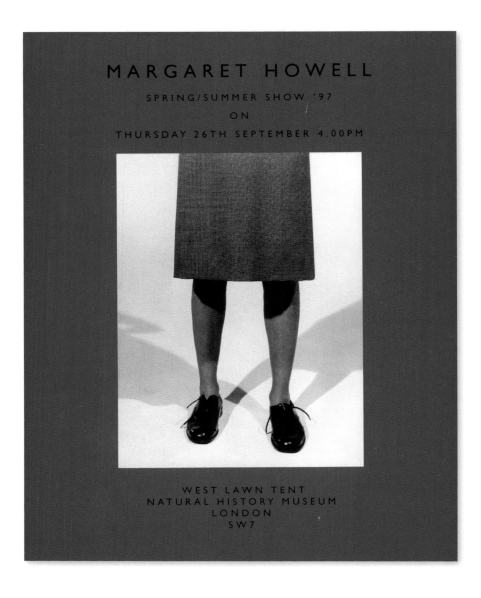

MARGARET HOWELL

SPRING/SUMMER SHOW '97

ON

THURSDAY 26TH SEPTEMBER 4.00PM

WEST LAWN TENT
NATURAL HISTORY MUSEUM
LONDON
SW7

Show
Promotional material

Date
circa 1987

Place
The House of Beauty
and Culture
34–36 Stamford Road
London

Format/Size
Postcard
14.5cm x 10cm
(5¾in x 4in)

John Moore

The House of Beauty & Culture store was established in the 1980s by shoe designer John Moore and acted as an experimental creative collective that included designers Christopher Nemeth, Judy Blame, Richard Torry and Dave Baby, as well as furniture makers Frick & Frack (Alan McDonald and Fritz Solomon). Situated in the East End of London, the wasteland panorama provided the perfect backdrop and defined the group's aesthetic. The designers used material others discarded. Nemeth famously made trousers from postal sacks, while Blame and Moore would regularly go scavenging on the banks of the River Thames.

 This raw ambience spilled over into the store's interior and stock. Frick & Frack made tables and shelves from railway sleepers, while Moore, who had trained at London's Cordwainers, hacked into a pair of shoes and patched them with leather offcuts. These shoes became a cult item. Moore, who died in 1989, was the archetype urban romantic: other high-heeled shoes featured a tractor-tyre sole or a squared toe, as seen on the promotional postcard.

Miu Miu

The models who walk in Miuccia Prada's Miu Miu show, including Stella Tennant, Kirsten Owen and Esther de Jong, are among the coolest girls on Planet Fashion. They wear sooty eye make-up and mussed-up hairdos. This collection which Prada titled "Blue genes" was as understated as the presentation on the stark white catwalk: clean and pared down, yet still a tad oddball. In sections called "Ship Boy" and "Gymnast Fishergirls", neat boxy jackets were teamed with cropped pants, chunky sweaters with big knickers and little white cotton shirts with full-length skirts. Prada loves kooky styling touches, especially the combination shown on the invitation, so those schoolgirl socks teamed with high heels were worn throughout the collection. Pretty floral chiffon mididresses were followed by sheer white dresses with visible, sensibly sized Bridget Jones-type underwear.

   The finale featured a series of plain dark sweaters teamed with ballgown skirts cut in heavy denim and tapestry fabrics, so long that the models were forced to hike them up.

Show
Spring/Summer
1997

Date/Time
31st October 1996
10am

Place
Pavilion
20 West 40th Street
New York

Format/Size
Card
28cm x 20cm (unfolded)
(11in x 8in)

Show
Spring/Summer
2009

Date/Time
30th October 2008

Place
Blahnik's Studio
49–51 Old Church
Street
London

Format/Size
Card
16cm x 22cm
(6in x 8½in)

Manolo Blahnik

One of the most coveted invitations of any season is not for a fashion show at all but the opportunity for select fashion editors to see (and even get to try on) the latest shoes by designer Manolo Blahnik. Over tea at Blahnik's Chelsea studio, cupboards would be dramatically opened to reveal shelves filled with his desirable shoes, but only the right foot of each design. For the lucky few, Blahnik himself would talk through each new style, explaining the flamboyant names he gives them with excitable, theatrical asides. This particular season, Blahnik favoured predominantly spike-thin high heels, although a self-confessed fan of the flat shoe, he also included a barely-there moccasin-style sandal called "Bavarese". Along with the strappy sandals and court shoes, he added a dramatic cutaway boot in slub silk and gold leather, "Kakona".

Blahnik's invitations are special for another reason as each one features an illustration by the man himself. This minimalist watercolour depicted the designer's new pointy toe shape.

Tom Binns

Irishman Tom Binns is a jewellery designer with a difference. His creations are as likely to take inspiration from Marcel Duchamp as Marlene Dietrich. Perhaps not surprisingly, Binns' anarchic assemblage approach brought him to the attention of Vivienne Westwood and Malcolm McLaren. In 1983, Binns accessorized the duo's "Punkature" collection (see also page 103) with what he described as "fluorescent rubber bits and pieces". McLaren referred to Binns as "a noble savage" and his designs certainly suggest an organic punk majesty; imagined long-lost jewels of some dispossessed royal family. A later collection would indeed collage Queen Elizabeth II's Crown Jewels with safety pins and chains.

Binns gained a loyal following among press and public alike (including Diana, Princess of Wales) and was soon creating seasonal collections. Despite the title "Future Fantastic", Binns modestly referred to this collection as "Latest Work". It included a mix of monumental-looking silver bracelets, metallic lace and Masai-style golden torques, referenced on the invitation.

Show
Spring/Summer
2009

Date/Time
29th September–5th October 2008

Place
Hotel Lotti Paris
The Michelangelo Suite
7 rue de Castiglione
Paris

Format/Size
Card
20cm x 13.5cm
(7¾in x 5¼in)

Hermès

During the 1980s Hermès, established in 1837 as an equestrian workshop, was going through something of a radical makeover. A young designer, Eric Bergère, was assigned the task to update the august French fashion house. His spirited viewpoint brought a sense of fun to the luxury label that drew it to the attention of young European stylists, who were enamoured by the heady combination of eccentricity, exclusivity and excess (a mink jogging suit or a suit fashioned from crocodile skin?). Bergère's designs were playful and played on the perceived jet-set lifestyle of the Hermès customer. For this show the Hermès afficionado was taken on an exotic safari with themes that included "the luxury of tranquillity", accessorized with hats, bags and shoes bordering on the cartoonesque. At this time Bergère's good friend Christian Lacroix was also playing sartorial high jinx. Together, the designers were dusting off the old image of the grand Parisian fashion houses.

Show
Spring/Summer
1988

Date/Time
20th October 1987
2.30pm

Place
Carrousel de Louvre
99 rue de Rivoli
Paris

Format/Size
Card, paper
23cm x 31cm
(9¼in x 12½in)

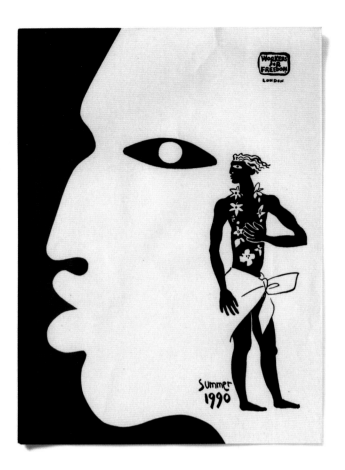
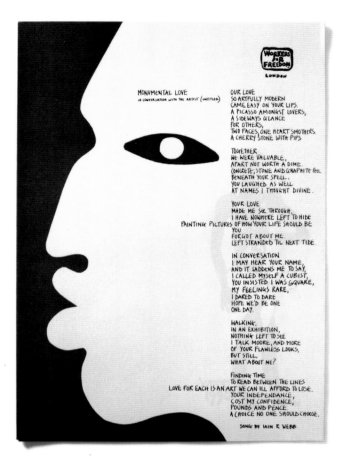

Workers for Freedom

When this collection was shown, Richard Nott and Graham Fraser were newly crowned Designers of the Year and the pair celebrated by hosting a glitzy "White" dinner at the same venue. The duo's brand of unpretentious, relaxed glamour in linen, cotton and silk garnered them a loyal following. This show included oversized shirts, circular skirts and waterfall ruffles. Many styles featured naive appliqué and embroidery, often handdrawn by Nott. Workers for Freedom catwalk presentations, produced by Mikel Rosen, featured carefully curated soundtracks incorporating specially commissioned poems, or in this case a song called "Monumental Love" (the words featured in the shownotes), performed by vocalist Jimmy Somerville. Other shows had featured paeans to Inuit and Aboriginal culture.

These programme notes welcome "A new decade. A new attitude. A new individualism". Certainly, Workers For Freedom situated themselves on the outskirts of the fashion industry, choosing the name of their label as a statement of intent. They sold the company in 2000. The pair live on the South Downs, where Nott now paints.

Show
Spring/Summer 1990

Date/Time
October 1989

Place
The Mall Galleries
The Mall
London

Format/Size
Paper
29.5cm x 21cm
(11¾in x 8¼in)

Rifat Ozbek

Show
Spring/Summer
1991

Date/Time
October 1990

Place
London

Format/Size
Card, CD
29.5cm x 21cm
(11¾in x 8¼in)

Music has always provided a crucial inspiration for designer Rifat Ozbek, so it seems appropriate that he should utilize a CD on this invitation. This collection, called "Afrodisia", brought together urban street-style sportswear with African culture (a look he returned to often). The invitation featured the model Lorraine Pascale, now best known as a TV celebrity chef, sporting the CD as an earring.

This mix of club-culture and ethnic influences has been key to the Ozbek brand since the designer graduated from St Martin's School of Art in 1977. Other collections by Ozbek have referenced Mexicana, Americana and the Russian ballet, which he unveiled in intimate salon presentations in his showroom for 20 or so invited guests. This collection was not shown on a catwalk but instead was captured in a short film directed by John Maybury. Ozbek drew huge inspiration from the subterranean London club scene, including The Daisy Chain at The Fridge nightclub in Brixton, South London.

Jean Paul Gaultier

This show was Gaultier's homage to *My Fair Lady*, specifically Cecil Beaton's beautifully costumed racetrack scene that featured in the film, hence the jokey cardboard cutout binoculars doubling as the invitation. The designer's catwalk zig-zagged throughout the location covered in fake grass. During the show the models paraded back and forth, this way and that, much to the annoyance of the photographers. Gaultier's designs also took inspiration from the Edwardian period in which the musical is set so that meant bustle-back trouser suits for ladies and corsets for the men teamed with top hats, picture hats and fluttering plumes. The designer mixed this up with modern body-conscious sportswear, S&M bondage and Latino colour. Flame-haired Eugenie Vincent, who modelled a light-up lampshade brassiere, shared the catwalk with Swedish Euro-pop group Army of Lovers, a greyhound, a dalmatian, and a toy-poodle in a tutu. For Gaultier, who emerged carrying a Jack Russell terrier, this was all part of the show, musical or otherwise.

Show
Spring/Summer
1992

Date/Time
18th October 1991
6pm

Place
Jardins Reserves des
Tuileries
Paris

Format/Size
Card, cord
25cm x 25cm
(10in x 10in)

Show
Autumn/Winter
2007–8

Date/Time
15th February 2007
7pm

Place
Club Row Building
Rochelle School
Arnold Circus
London

Format/Size
Card, ribbon
16cm x 21cm
(6½in x 8½in)

Giles

The badger mask invitation and giant porcupine quills poking from the backdrop were a clue that for this collection Giles Deacon was going back to nature. From the first dress on the catwalk, made from sheepskins roughly stitched together, the designer confirmed that he was taking his inspiration from the great outdoors. This included a deep forest colour palette, primitive-looking prints and outsize organic knits that appeared to grow around the models like vines around the trunk of a tree. But Deacon still couldn't resist some sophisticated couture fabrics such as duchess satin, but this time he coloured it vivid grass green. The designer went wild with accessories: fluffy rooster feathers sprouted from ankle straps of high-heeled sandals, while a collar of pheasant feathers standing 1.2 metres (4 feet) tall, completely obliterated one poor model's features. An outfit from this collection earned Deacon the prestigious 2007 Dress of the Year award at the Fashion Museum, Bath, selected by fashion writer Hywel Davies.

Jean Paul Gaultier

The masked models that crept stealthily around Jean Paul Gaultier's catwalk were photo-fit likenesses for Arthur J. Raffles, the Victorian gentleman thief created by E.W. Hornung. The previous evening, the boxing ring staging had been the setting for Régine Chopinot's ballet KOK, costumed by Gaultier. This show began with four male models disguised in false moustaches, dressed entirely in creamy white, standing motionless on the revolving set. Their outfits were a mélange of historic tail coats, corsets, cotton gloves and quilted waistcoats that looked part-fencing kit, part-flak jacket. Another military touch was officer's stripes outlining cavalry-style stirrup pants. The designer added sparkle with sequinned jean jackets, Lurex tuxedos, PVC raincoats and blousy satin opera scarves.

The show featured Brit model Martine Houghton, who walked on both Gaultier's mens- and womenswear catwalks. Actor Peter Coyote, who was in the audience, dubbed this collection, "fashion of the future". Gaultier returned to the boxing ring again in 2010 (see also page 267).

Show
Menswear
Autumn/Winter
1989–90

Date/Time
5th February 1989
12.30pm

Place
Grande Halle de la Villette
221 avenue Jean Jaurès
Paris

Format/Size
Paper
28.5cm x 20cm
(11in x 8in)

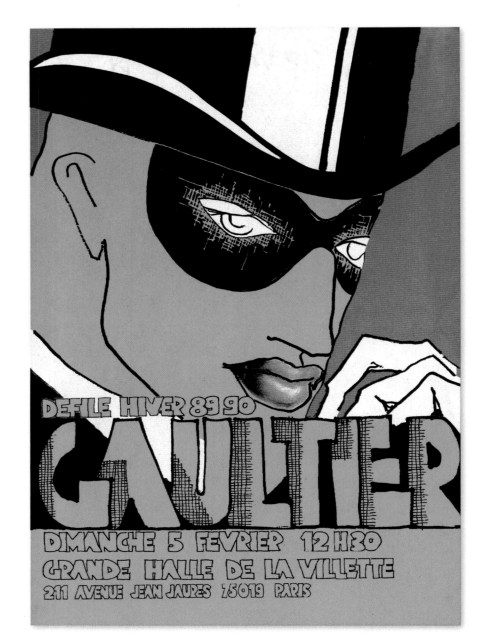

DEFILE HIVER 89 90
GAULTIER
DIMANCHE 5 FEVRIER 12 H 30
GRANDE HALLE DE LA VILLETTE
211 AVENUE JEAN JAURES 75019 PARIS

Isaac Mizrahi

Show
Spring/Summer
1997

Date/Time
October 1996

Place
New York

Format/Size
Card, elastic
21cm x 22cm
(8in x 8½in)

Designers often leave gifts on the seats at shows but not all of them quite so egocentric as this mask. The headband became a trademark for Mizrahi and he can be seen sporting it in the 1995 film *Unzipped*. During the making of his Autumn/Winter 1994 collection Mizrahi allowed his boyfriend, film director Douglas Keeve, to document the process involved in building a collection and catwalk show. It reveals behind-the-scenes moments, including the designer's inspirations – Mary Tyler Moore, Nanook of the North and the 1962 movie *What Ever Happened to Baby Jane?* At this time he also produced a series of illustrated comic books depicting the "Adventures of Sandee The Supermodel" and a designer called "Yvesaac", who looked remarkably like Mizrahi, bandana and all! As Mizrahi took his bows for this show, appropriately to "You Gotta Have A Gimmick" from the musical *Gypsy*, some guests donned the mask, as did models, Kirsty Hume, Christina Cruz, Chandra North and Amy Wesson, who posed backstage for photographer Roxanne Lowit.

Blumarine

Although this Blumarine show started with slick updates on the classic Parisian beatnik look, it was the printed bias-cut dresses that caught the girly mood defining this particular show season in Milan. Not surprisingly, given her nickname "The Queen of Roses", the label's designer Anna Molinari offered endless variations on the rose print. The flower also featured scaled-up large on the backdrop and projected onto the catwalk during the show's finale. However, the Blumarine girl likes to mix things up so this season Molinari added leopard print. Model Naomi Campbell appeared, wearing the leopard mask, as seen on the invitation, teamed with a matching frilly, flirty chiffon dress. Campbell modelled alongside Milla Jovovich (yet to make her big break into films), who wore a leopard-print bikini and cool British posh girls, Stella Tennant and Iris Palmer. At the end of the show there were more flowers: as Molinari took her bow, her fans threw roses onto the catwalk.

Show
Spring/Summer
1997

Date/Time
October 1996

Place
The Fiera
Strada Statale del
Sempione, 28
Milan

Format/Size
Card
11cm x 6.5cm
(6½in x 4½in)

Show
Spring/Summer
1997

Date/Time
29th October 1996
5pm

Place
Pavilion
20 West 40th Street
New York

Format/Size
Card
6cm x 16.5cm
(2¼in x 6½in)

Vivienne Tam

The mood for fashion inspired by Orientalism was already bubbling on the catwalks of Europe (with Miuccia Prada showing a much-lauded collection), so Chinese-born Vivienne Tam was a designer to go see during New York Fashion Week, which traditionally fell at the end of the season. Tam's designs were never overly showy and she captured the mood for pretty spaghetti-strap frocks in delicate blossom print fabrics. More overt were her versions of authentic Cheongsam dresses sparsely decorated with bamboo print or embroidered dragons. The designer's use of brocade and sequins added further glamour and was a foil for uniform-style tailored pieces. Posh Brit "It" girl Iris Palmer modelled, along with Carolyn Park-Chapman. With their hair clipped into topknots with metal headbands and smudgy cat's-eye make-up, the look was a modern-day version of a geisha.

 Tam's recent optical catwalk antics include a dress featuring a portrait of US President Barack Obama sporting shades.

FLYTE OSTELL

Flyte Ostell

Ellis Flyte and Richard Ostell, who formed their label in 1992, had previously been fêted as designers in their own right: Flyte for her lingerie-style looks, while Ostell had made understatement his raison d'être. The duo were not fans of fashion that changes every six months, instead preferring to create effortless, unfussy garments that would become wardrobe classics, worn with pieces from other collections and seasons. Their unstructured silhouette provided an alternative to the working wardrobe of jackets and suits and the pair became an immediate hit with the fashion industry and customers alike. The dreamy, wistful image featured on the invitation captured the duo's favoured mood – layered pieces cut from luxury fabrication (silk, organza, satin, jersey and cashmere) were integral to the Flyte Ostell look. At this time the designers were extending their range by creating a capsule collection for Evans, the high street chainstore catering for plus size women.

Show
Spring/Summer
1996

Date/Time
23rd–24th October 1995

Place
Royal College of Art
Kensington Gore
London

Format/Size
Card
15cm x 15cm
(6in x 6in)

17/10:9h30

Show
Spring/Summer
1996

Date/Time
17th October 1995
9.30am

Place
Carrousel du Louvre
Salle Soufflot
rue de Rivoli
Paris

Format/Size
Card, CD
12.5cm x 12.5cm
(5in x 5in)

Barbara Bui

Barbara Bui staged her first fashion show in Paris in 1987, opening a boutique just a year later, on rue Étienne Marcel. Her initial designs were handcrafted pieces in leather and suede, which continued to feature as signature fabrics in her collections, reinforcing the sense of luxury that pervades her designs. At the core of Bui's philosophy is an androgynous sensibility, a laid-back elegance that has been dubbed "rock chic". It is perhaps not surprising then that the designer should choose to send her guests a CD as an invitation, the cover of which features a graphic close-up of 1960s model Twiggy's trademark spidery false lashes.

Bui has since released two compilation CDs, *Barbara Bui Café Vol. 1 and 2*, featuring electronica mixed by DJ Emmanuel Santarromana. However, this complimentary CD was credited to Armand Amar. A later music-orientated collaboration between Bui and Californian brand Frends produced a pair of leather headphones decorated with metal studs.

Betty Jackson

Despite the early Sunday morning start, Betty Jackson's brand of bona fide relaxed glamour seduced her bleary-eyed guests. This collection, like the invitation, was a collage of old and new inspirations reflecting the 25 years Jackson had been showing on the London Fashion Week catwalk.

    New touches included a furry top belted with a crocodile bow, blousy ruffles and a bold wood grain print. Jackson mixed up chrysanthemum and poppy prints, distressed velvet and soft angora knits in surprising colourways: baby blue, chocolate, egg-yolk yellow, tobacco, lemon, grey and poppy red. Pencil skirts and softer dirndl skirts (both with practical pockets) were worn with shawl wraps, a little wool dress accessorized with a rucksack. There was a Japanese mood to the artful drapery in effortless black dresses. Styled by Lucy Ewing, fashion director of *Sunday Times Style* magazine, the collection was given an edgy look with wrinkled wool stockings and patent platform court shoes in lavender and turquoise.

Show
Autumn/Winter
2009–10

Date/Time
22nd February 2009
9.15am

Place
British Fashion Council
Tent
Natural History Museum
Cromwell Road
London

Format/Size
Card
21cm x 14.5cm
(8¼in x 5¾in)

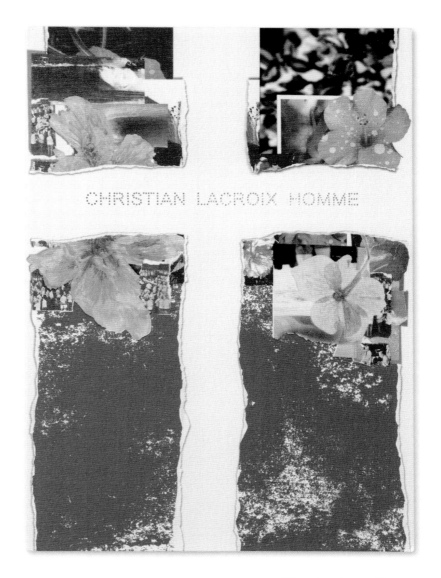

Show
Menswear
Spring/Summer
2013

Date/Time
27 June 2012
7.30pm

Place
Hotel de Brossier
12 rue Charlot
Paris

Format/Size
Card
21cm x 15cm
(8¼in x 6in)

Christian Lacroix

In 2009 Christian Lacroix presented his final haute couture collection. Then, in 2013, Sacha Walckhoff, Lacroix's former right-hand man, stepped into the designer's shoes to create this menswear collection for the label. Walckhoff described how the genesis of the collection came from an encounter with a young surfer-cum-artist selling skateboards on Venice Beach, California. The meeting not only dictated the sunny yellow and blue palette but also flamboyant collage prints directly inspired by the young man's artworks (the collage featured on the invitation appeared on a classic white shirt). Walckhoff also used this encounter to determine a younger, more energetic, contemporary customer for the brand, who would be excited by the strong visual legacy of Lacroix. The silhouette was constructed from sporty separates including zippy bomber jackets, cropped trousers and T-shirts.

In the same year Lacroix returned to design a collection of 18 couture ensembles for the house of Schiaparelli.

John Galliano

Against a backdrop of flashing neon tube lights in varying shades of pink the first model stomped out onto the catwalk to the sound of actress Tatum O'Neal singing "My Name Is Tallulah" from the soundtrack of the Alan Parker's all-child musical *Bugsy Malone*. Dressed to resemble the collage illustration featured on the invitation, in frills, poufs of tulle and lace, pearl chokers, ankle socks and with their underpinnings on display, Galliano's girls resembled freaky Victorian china doll crossed with Brooke Shields in *Pretty Baby*. However, there was nothing innocent about the collection; these fondant-coloured confections were sweet, but disturbing. With heavily pencilled eyebrows, overly rouged cheeks and hair piled high, with tiny boater hats perched on top, Galliano teased with a look that was part-Marie Antoinette as bucolic milkmaid at Hameau de la Reine, part-Benny Hill travesty. Meanwhile, the soundtrack merrily clashed Haysi Fantayzee's "Shiny Shiny" with Lieutenant Pigeon's "Mouldy Old Dough".

Show
Spring/Summer
2004

Date/Time
11th October 2003
8pm

Place
Théâtre de l'Empire
37 Avenue de Wagram
Paris

Format/Size
Card
21cm x 29.5cm
(8in x 11¾in)

Show
Menswear
Spring/Summer 2011

Date/Time
22nd September 2010
11.30am

Place
Navy Board Rooms
Somerset House
The Strand
London

Format/Size
Card
14.5cm x 21cm
(6¾in x 8¼in)

E. Tautz

Fronting the primetime BBC TV series *The Great British Sewing Bee*, the designer Patrick Grant has become something of a TV celebrity. This presentation in the stately Navy Rooms at Somerset House was the antithesis of attention-seeking catwalk antics. Grant talked the assembled guests through each outfit. As menswear is traditionally all about the detail, this style of show suited the brand (established by Edward Tautz in 1867), with Grant able to highlight specifics of fabrication or the cut of a tapered double-breasted blazer.

Although the collection was firmly fixed in its Savile Row heritage, there were obvious attempts by the designer to offer a fashion edge: tapered trousers were cropped to reveal a bare ankle (even with formal brogue or Oxford shoes), dapper bow ties were worn with shorts and linen jackets were softer in construction. As the collaged invitation showed, the collection had a nostalgic spirit: *The Talented Mr. Ripley* meets *Brighton Rock*.

Stephen Jones

The venue for Jones' birthday party, hosted by friends Fiona Dealey and Vicki Sarge, was the perfect setting for the milliner who has dedicated his life to creating hats that provide the extravagant finishing touch to any outfit. The Oliver Messel Suite was created by the eponymous theatre designer in the 1950s and is a mix of elaborate and exotic that might well describe any of Jones' delightful creations. Past occupants have included Marlene Dietrich, Noël Coward, Elizabeth Taylor (it was here that she honeymooned with Richard Burton) and Sylvester Stallone and so, not surprisingly, the look is ultra-luxurious with an interior featuring a pagan altar fireplace, painted friezes, chintz drapes and gold-leaf toilet seats.

Esteemed fashion illustrator Lawrence Mynott created this unique "Mad Hatter" invitation for the designer who is one of fashion's most-loved characters. Mynott's work also featured on the cover of *Hats: An Anthology*, a book that accompanied Jones' V&A exhibition, another hot ticket.

Show
50th Birthday Party

Date/Time
27 May 2007
7pm–9pm

Place
Oliver Messel Suite
The Dorchester
53 Park Lane
London

Format/Size
Card
12.5cm x 17.5cm
(5in x 7in)

Guido Palau

Show
40th Birthday Party

Date/Time
31st January 2002
8.30pm–3am

Place
The Roost
Sandringham Road
London

Format/Size
Card
14.5cm x 21cm
(5¾in x 8¼in)

Guido Palau is described by British *Vogue* as "the world's most in-demand hairdresser", so this was a coveted invitation. However, rather than choose a swanky West End nightclub, Palau plumped for a revamped public house in a less than salubrious part of London's East End. But then the hairdresser had achieved fame in the 1990s as part of the British grunge contingent (including photographers David Sims and Corinne Day, model Kate Moss and stylist Anna Cockburn), which literally flipped the fashion industry's definition of glamour and beauty overnight – hence the punk-style graphics seen here. The party was housed over several floors, with guests meandering through quirkily decorated rooms. On the ground floor, Palau and his fabulous fashion-pack friends danced themselves dizzy to favourite disco tunes. In 2000, Palau launched his acclaimed book *Heads: Hair by Guido* with another invitation-only party at the achingly refined Calvin Klein store on Madison Avenue in New York – a tad different from this spirited British affair.

Hamish Bowles

For his 50th birthday celebrations US *Vogue* European editor-at-large Hamish Bowles went transatlantic with parties in both America and the UK. In Long Island, New York *Vogue* editor Anna Wintour threw a party with a Great Gatsby theme. Bowles, who is known for his sartorial sharpness and is a regular on Best Dressed Lists, commissioned Ralph Lauren to make him a reproduction of the pink suit worn by Robert Redford in the 1974 version of *The Great Gatsby* movie (Lauren had designed the original costumes), which was worn with a lilac satin tie. The pastel theme continued, from the illustration of Bowles on this invitation to firework displays in the English countryside, where there were no less than three more parties. These included a costume ball dedicated to Cecil Beaton (one of Bowles' heroes), hosted by designer Jasper Conran, followed the next evening by a black tie dinner and a *fête de champagne* the following afternoon.

Show
50th Birthday Party

Date/Time
21st July 2013
1pm

Place
Hanham Court Gardens
Gloucestershire

Format/Size
Card
15cm x 20.5cm
(6in x 8in)

PICTURE CREDITS

INDEX

AUTHOR'S ACKNOWLEDGEMENTS

I would like to thank the following for allowing me to rifle through their personal collections and loaning their much-treasured invitations: Lina Berardi, Adrian Clark, Nicola Copping, Wendy Dagworthy, Sarah Dallas, Hywel Davies, Gregory Davis, Sally Dennis, Vanessa Denza, Yvonne Gold, Andrew Groves, David Holah, David Kappo, Charlie Porter, Frances Ronaldson, Liz Shirley, Lou Stoppard, Stevie Stewart and Roger Tredre.

I would also like to thank the following for their assistance in sourcing invitations and help with additional research: Sugar Ansari, Sarah Barnes, Susanne Bartsch, Tanel Bedrossiantz, Antonio Berardi, Eric Bergère, Cally Blackman, Murray Blewett, Hamish Bowles and team especially Lauren Sanchez, Martin Brading, William Brown at Old Town, Antoni Burakowski, Melissa Caplan, Robert Cary-Williams, Joe Casely-Hayford, Nick Coleman, Jasper Conran and team especially Neil Penlington, Michael Costiff, Natasha Cowan, Simon Cryer, Helen David, Fiona Dealey, Sean Ellis, Katy England, Franklin Ettedgui, Isabel Ettedgui, Lucy Ewing, Jonathan Faiers, Cliff Fleiser at Tom Ford International, Robert Forrest, Joe Fountain at Manolo Blahnik, Susannah Frankel, Graham Fraser, Sam Gainsbury, Jean Paul Gaultier, Gill Griffiths, Rosemary Harden and Elaine Uttley at the Fashion Museum, Bath, David Hiscock, Hongyi Huang at Alexander McQueen, Betty Jackson, Sarah Jones, Stephen Jones, Kamran Khavari, Ninivah Khomo, Ben Kirchhoff, William Kohler-Nudelmont, Michelle Lederer at Calvin Klein, Mandi Lennard, Stephen Linard, Andrew Logan, Frédérique Lorca, Julien Macdonald, Russell Marsh, John Maybury, Laura McCuaig and Frances Knight-Jacobs at Vivienne Westwood, Edward Meadham, Suzy Menkes, Thomas Miller, Jelka Music, Sophia Neophitou, Christina Newton, Terence Nolder, Richard Nott, Peter O'Brien, Perry Ogden, Jo Ortmans, Peppe Orru, Richard Ostell, Rifat Ozbek, Tina Patel, Kerrie-Anne Pritchard at Christopher Kane, Zandra Rhodes, Gordon Richardson, John Richmond, Alison Roberts, John Rocha, Mikel Rosen, Fiona Rushton, Catherine Schiffers and Pauline Vilbert at Hermes, Barrie Sharpe, Imogen Snell, Dean Stephen at Tom Binns, Kim Stringer, Paula Sutton, Fiorella Terenzi, Julian Vogel and team at Modus PR especially Sarah Bruce-Green, and Marysia Woroniecka.

I especially thank Caroline Evans for her expert knowledge and advice, and Karen Cannell and April Calahan at FIT Archives for the loan of their exquisite historic invitations. I would not have been able to make this book without the archive material of Chris Moore and his team at www.catwalking.com specifically Maxine Millar, or the digital documentation of Elsa Klensch and CNN Style, Fashion Channel, Tim Blanks at Style.com and Nick Knight and his inspirational team at SHOWstudio. I would also like to express my gratitude to CINEMIX.com for providing the soundtrack for the making of this book.

It has been a delight to work with Mabel Chan and the team at Carlton Publishing Group especially my editors, Venetia Bartleet and Lisa Dyer, whom I would like to thank for keeping this show so skillfully on the road and making the experience so inviting. And I would particularly like to thank Anna Sui for her kind words and enthusiasm for the project (and for sending me invitations to her fashion shows over the years).

As ever I could not have done this project without my partner Mark Clarke who has had to endure for far too long the "delirium of dressing". I dedicate this book to The Artist.

Please join us for
an after show drink in
"Aggies bar "
opposite our exhibition
stand (B2)

The Women's Committee
invites you
for a
special evening
of
Zandra Rhodes 79
Chinese Collection
presented by Saks-Jandel
to benefit
The Corcoran Gallery of Art
Wednesday evening 12. september 79
17th Street & New York Avenue N.W.
Washington D.C.
6·30 pm cocktails for 8·00 pm show.

ANNA SUI SPRING 1996

KINKY GERLINKY

HOLLY FULTON
AUTUMN/WINTER 2014

DIOR

Antonio Aligi
'SPONTANEOUS'
piece of work for AW2008.

LORD ARTHUR SAVILE'S CRIME